Betty Crocker

30 minute meals for diabetes

D1459930

WILEY
WILEY PUBLISHING, INC.

General Mills

Publisher, Cookbooks: Maggie Gilbert and Lynn Vettel
Senior Cookbook Editor: Cheri Olerud
Recipe Development and Testing: Betty Crocker Kitchens
Photography: General Mills Photography Studios and Image Library
Photographer: Andy Swarbrick (Interior & Cover)
Food Stylists: Cindy Lund

Wiley Publishing, Inc.

Publisher: Natalie Chapman
Executive Editor: Anne Ficklen
Senior Editorial Assistant: Charleen Barila
Production Manager: Michael Olivo
Senior Production Editor: Jacqueline Beach
Cover Design: Suzanne Sunwoo
Art Director: Tai Blanche
Manufacturing Manager: Kevin Watt
Photography Art Direction: Judy Meyer
Prop Stylist: Michele Joy

The Betty Crocker Kitchens seal guarantees success in your kitchen. Every recipe has been tested in America's Most Trusted Kitchens™ to meet our high standards of reliability, easy preparation and great taste.

FIND MORE GREAT IDEAS AT
BettyCrocker.com

This book is printed on acid-free paper. ∞

For general information on our other products and services or for technical support, please contact our Customer Care Department within the United States at (800) 762-2974, outside the United States at (317) 572-3993 or fax (317) 572-4002.

Wiley also publishes its books in a variety of electronic formats. Some content that appears in print may not be available in electronic books. For more information about Wiley products, visit our web site at **www.wiley.com**.

Library of Congress Cataloging-in-Publication Data:

Crocker, Betty.
   Betty Crocker 30-minute meal for diabetes / Betty Crocker.
      p. cm.
   Includes index.
   ISBN 978-0-470-19117-0 (cloth)
   1. Diabetes—Diet therapy—Recipes. I. Title. II. Title: 30-minute meal for diabetes. III. Title: Thirty-minute meal for diabetes.
   RC662.C754 2008
   641.5'6314—dc22

                           2007044565

Manufactured in China

10 9 8 7 6 5 4 3 2 1

Cover Photos: Broccoli-Cheese Soup (page 206), Caribbean Turkey Stew (page 174), Chicken–Wild Rice Salad with Dried Cherries (page 146), Chicken Linguine Alfredo (page 198)

Dear Friends,

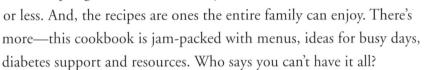

Just because you have diabetes doesn't mean you have to give up one of the greatest joys in life—the joy of eating. All it takes is a little planning and really tasty recipes at your fingertips. Betty Crocker serves up easy, taste-tempting main dishes all ready in 30 minutes, or less. And, the recipes are ones the entire family can enjoy. There's more—this cookbook is jam-packed with menus, ideas for busy days, diabetes support and resources. Who says you can't have it all?

Easy main dishes for people with diabetes? Who knew you could still eat pizza and pasta? Who knew that by counting carbs, you would feel better and that your whole family could reap the rewards of eating for diabetes? Betty knew—and now you and your family can enjoy these diabetes-friendly meals any night of the week! Try out fun, new snacks in the Mini Meals chapter. If yours is a two-person household, the recipes in Cooking for Two will be right up your alley. Love traditional foods? Try the recipes in the Traditional Favorites chapter—carbohydrates, calories and fat have been reduced while keeping great taste.

The good news is that it is possible to live well and eat well when you have diabetes—especially when you have the right recipes and the best information at your fingertips. Here's to eating well!

Betty Crocker

Contents

Eat Well for Good Health

Most people agree that eating is one of the great joys in life. Having diabetes doesn't have to change that. Viewing diabetes as an opportunity to prepare and eat the best possible foods to maintain your body may help you with the daily challenge of diabetes. With experience, you'll be able to modify recipes or situations to fit your needs. Eventually, you may even like your new way of eating better than the old way. An added benefit is you'll feel better, both physically and mentally, and the whole family can reap the rewards of eating well.

The Role of Carbohydrates

Foods contain three nutrients: carbohydrate, protein and fat. Carbohydrates are necessary for good nutrition, but they raise your blood glucose level, so pay attention to how much of them you eat. They provide important nutrients, vitamins, minerals and give your body the energy it needs. Without carbohydrates, your body cannot function properly. And, it's wise to eat carbohydrate foods in moderation to avoid excess calories and weight gain.

Where's the Carbohydrate?

There are many sources of carbohydrates. These foods contain our body's favorite energy source, carbohydrate:

- Fruit and fruit juices
- Cereal, pasta, rice and other grains
- Breads, crackers and rolls
- Milk and yogurt
- Vegetables
- Sugar, honey, jam, jelly and syrup

Cakes, pies, bars, cookies, candy and **ice cream** contain carbohydrates and in addition, contain fat. So do snacks like chips, buttered popcorn and crackers. Fortunately, low-fat and fat-free versions of these popular snack foods are widely available.

Pizza, soups, stews, pasta dishes, **casseroles** and **sandwiches** are examples of foods that contain carbohydrate, protein and fat.

Together, you and your registered dietitian will determine how many carbohydrates to eat each day, and the best way to space carbs throughout the day so you get the energy you need without overwhelming your body's insulin supply. Since your body "runs" on carbohydrates, every meal and snack needs to contain some.

Carbohydrate Counting

Carbohydrate counting is a tool to help control blood glucose and helps you select the amount of carbohydrate recommended by your health care provider for a well-balanced diet. Carbohydrate is measured in grams. A gram is a small unit of weight in the metric system. The trick to carbohydrate counting is to know how many carbohydrate grams you eat. A typical diabetes food plan includes 3 to 5 Carbohydrate Choices per meal. Snacks are usually 1 or 2 Carbohydrate Choices.

Why Is Counting Carbohydrates So Important?

Carbohydrates affect blood glucose levels more than any other nutrient. Eating even small amounts of carbohydrate will make your blood glucose rise. Eating large amounts of carbohydrate will cause a greater rise.

Choices: An Easy Way to Count Carbohydrates

Diabetes guidelines use a simple way to plan foods, called *carbohydrate counting.* All you have to actually

---

What Is a Carbohydrate Choice?

A Carbohydrate Choice is a serving of food that contains 15 grams of carbohydrate. This is the approximate amount of carbohydrate in one serving of: Potato, Rice, Bread, Cereal, Milk, Apple.

1 Carbohydrate choice = **1** = **15** grams of Carbohydrate

If you eat two apples, it counts as 2 Carbohydrate Choices. If you eat one slice of bread and one cup of milk, that also counts as 2 Carbohydrate Choices. Your customized food plan will include the right number of Carbohydrate Choices for you.

count are the carbohydrate grams. The total amount of carbohydrate you need daily is divided into sets of 15 grams each. One set of 15 grams of carbohydrate equals 1 Carbohydrate Choice. The number fifteen is used because 15 grams of carbohydrate is the approximate amount of carbohydrate in one serving of bread, milk or fruit, standard foods in the American diet.

Spread across meals and snacks, your customized meal plan includes the right number of Carbohydrate Choices for you. You can work with your dietitian to add in the right amount of protein and fat to round out the carbohydrates you're eating.

If a food has 5 or more grams of fiber, subtract the total fiber grams from the total carbohydrate grams before determining the number of Carbohydrate Choices. It's that simple!

Essential for Good Health

In addition to carbohydrates, several nutrients are needed every day to maintain optimal health. It's important to balance your intake of **protein**, **fat** and **carbohydrate** as part of a healthy diet. Just as eating too many carbs may lead to excess calories and weight, a diet too high in protein and fat but low in carbohydrate won't provide your body with the energy and balanced nutrition it needs for proper functioning. Bottom line, use moderation.

PROTEIN is found in meats, poultry, fish, milk and other dairy products, eggs, dried peas and beans. Starch and vegetables also have small amounts of protein. Your body uses protein for energy, growth and maintenance. Protein provides four calories per gram. Your dietitian will help you determine how much protein is right for your body. Five to seven ounces of protein per day is typically recommended. Whenever you have the choice, drink fat-free (skim) milk, eat low-fat cheeses, yogurt and puddings. Also use low-fat ingredients for cooking and baking.

FAT is found in butter, margarine, oils, salad dressings, nuts, seeds, cheese, meat, fish, poultry, snack foods, ice cream, cookies and many desserts. Your body needs some fat for good nutrition, just as it needs protein and carbohydrate. Fat provides nine calories per gram, more than twice the calories found in carbohydrate or protein.

Excess calories from fat are easily stored in the body, and eating too much fat can contribute to heart disease.

Certain types of fat are better for you than others. There are three different types of fat: **saturated, monounsaturated** and **polyunsaturated**. Health professionals recommend eating less of the saturated fats found in meats; dairy products; coconut, palm and palm kernel oils; and fats that are hard at room temperature. Saturated fats have been proven to raise blood cholesterol levels. The best fats are monounsaturated fats found in canola oil, olive oil, nuts and avocados. The polyunsaturated fats found in corn oil, soybean oil and sunflower oil are also good choices.

FIBER is necessary to maintain a healthy digestive tract and to help lower blood cholesterol levels. Experts recommend at least 25 grams of fiber daily. To get enough fiber each day, be sure to include:

- **Whole-grain** breads, cereals, bran, rice, pasta and other whole-grain products
- **Vegetables** and fruits, especially those with edible skins, seeds and hulls
- **Legumes** (dried beans and peas) and nuts

WATER is essential for good health. Experts generally recommend at least eight glasses of water daily.

VITAMINS help release energy from the fuel sources of carbohydrate, protein and fat. Your vision, hair, skin and bone strength all depend on the vitamins that come from the foods you eat. The more variety in your diet, the more likely you are to get all the vitamins your body needs.

MINERALS help your body with many functions. Iron, for example, a mineral that carries much-needed oxygen to your body cells, is in great demand. Calcium is the key to strong bones and teeth, and potassium is important for proper nerve and muscle function.

Five Simple Secrets to Manage Diabetes

Managing diabetes is the top priority. The goal of food planning is to keep blood glucose levels close to normal. By making just a few simple changes, you can help control blood glucose and achieve a healthy diet. Five ways to successfully manage your diabetes:

1 Eat Breakfast

Breakfast sets the stage for the rest of the day in terms of energy and nutrition. People who eat breakfast tend to have healthier diets, ones that contain more vitamins, minerals and fiber and less fat. Breakfast eaters are also more apt to have better weight control.

2 Don't Skip Meals

Skipping meals makes it difficult to maintain constant blood glucose levels. To make matters worse, people often end up overeating at the next meal. So keep to your meal plan, and for times when this isn't possible, talk to your dietitian to find appropriate snack choices to hold you over until you can eat your next meal.

3 Plan Meals and Snacks

Planning meals and snacks seems overwhelming at first, but in time, you'll be an expert on what foods work best for you. If you don't plan, you may find yourself eating what's available and that may not be the best food for you. In each meal, include a little protein from lean meats, nuts and low-fat dairy foods.

4 Control Portion Sizes

One way to control portion sizes is to use the **Plate System,** developed by the American Diabetes System. See box that illustrates it.

5 Exercise

One of the best things you can do for yourself is to find the physical activity that's right for you, then commit to it every day. Exercise helps lower blood pressure, improves blood cholesterol level and controls weight. For people with diabetes, there is an added benefit: Regular physical activity helps lower blood glucose levels by making the body's cells more sensitive to insulin. And for people at risk for diabetes, exercise can even help prevent the disease from developing.

In Your Kitchen

You can reduce the fat, calories and sodium plus add flavor where it counts the most, in your kitchen. Here's how:

- **Cut down on total fat and saturated fat.** When you use fat, think liquid. Use canola or olive oil rather than solid butter, margarine or shortening.

The Plate System

This easy trick lets you visually gauge each plate of food for nutritional balance—even restaurant meals. Here's how it works: Pretend your plate is divided in half. Then divide one of those halves into two equal sections:

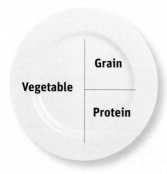

- **One-half plate** = Non-starchy Vegetables (like spinach, broccoli, cauliflower, eggplant, tomatoes, asparagus, romaine lettuce).

- **One-fourth plate** = 1 serving Meat or Other Protein (like egg or tofu).

- **One-fourth plate** = Bread/Grain (like bread, rice, tortillas, cereal) or Starchy Vegetables (like potatoes, corn, beans, lentils).

Sample Dinner: 1 serving skinless chicken breast (protein); 1 small sweet potato (starch); 1 serving lettuce/tomato salad and 1 serving steamed broccoli (non-starchy veggies). For more, see "Rate Your Plate" at www.diabetes.org.

- **Cook without adding fat.** Braise, steam, poach or bake food. Grilling, broiling and using a table-top grill are also good because they allow fat to drip off.
- **Reduce cholesterol.** Try to use egg whites and egg substitutes instead of whole eggs. Also eat more cholesterol-lowering foods like oats and barley.
- **Select whole grains.** Use whole wheat pasta, couscous, brown rice, bulgur wheat, millet, quinoa. Use whole wheat bread and buns for sandwiches.
- **Eat colorful foods, like vegetables and fruits.** Selecting the most colorful fruits and vegetables usually means that they're higher in vitamins, minerals and phytonutrients.
- **Add legumes and beans** to soups, stews and stir-fries.
- **Pick no-salt-added** or low-sodium broth when you need to reduce sodium. Don't add salt at the table and don't cook potatoes, pasta or rice in salted water.
- **Boost the amount of potassium you eat** to balance out the sodium, including peaches, tuna, beans, spinach and tomatoes.

Nutrition in the Recipes

Fats: Canola and olive oils are called for throughout the book, chosen for their heart-wise and health-wise benefits—they're great fats to use for stir-frying and cooking.

Dairy: Skim milk is used—an easy way to cut fat. Depending on the fat and calorie content of each dish, the recipes contain either fat-free or reduced-fat cream cheese and sour cream.

Eggs: Because eggs contain many nutrients, they're called for first, but you're given a choice of egg whites or egg substitute, if you prefer to reduce the cholesterol—the recipes work well with any of the three.

When the nutrition content of recipes was calculated, see guidelines on page 218:

THE HEALTHY DIABETES PANTRY

Having a wide variety of the right ingredients on hand in your cupboard, refrigerator and freezer offers tremendous flexibility for preparing fresh, easy and great-tasting lower-calorie, lower-fat recipes. This pantry list covers the basics of good-for-you cooking, with room to add your favorites.

Fresh Produce:

Any fruit or vegetable in season

Broccoli

Cabbage

Carrots

Cucumbers

Garlic

Onions

Potatoes

Salad greens (any variety)

Spinach and other leafy greens

Sweet potatoes

Apples

Bananas

Berries

Grapes

Melons

Oranges, tangerines or grapefruit

Dairy:

Fat-free (skim) or low-fat (1%) milk

Fat-free sour cream

Plain fat-free yogurt

Flavored fat-free yogurt

Trans-fat-free margarine

Reduced-fat cream cheese (Neufchâtel)

Low-fat or reduced-fat cheese

Meats/Poultry/Fish:

Well-trimmed beef, pork and lamb cuts ("loin")

Skinless chicken and turkey

All types of shellfish and fish, especially fatty types (such as salmon, tuna)

Lean cold cuts (such as sliced roast turkey or beef)

Low-fat sausages (such as turkey)

Cereals/Pastas/Grains

Whole-grain cereals

Old-fashioned oats

Whole-grain pasta

Quinoa, whole wheat couscous, bulgur wheat

Snacks:

Whole-grain crackers or flatbreads

Rice crackers

Whole wheat pretzels

Plain popcorn or low-fat microwave popcorn

Fig bars

Graham crackers

Canned and Bottled Goods:

Reduced-sodium broths and soups

Canned beans (such as black, canellini, chili, kidney beans)

Canned no-salt-added tomatoes

Fat-free bean dip

Canned fruits (in water or fruit juice)

Oils and Dressings/Sauces:

Canola or soybean oil

Olive oil

Peanut butter

Low-fat or fat-free salad dressings

Balsamic vinegar and/or other flavored vinegars

Pasta sauce

Salsa

Frozen Foods:

Soy-protein burgers and crumbles (look for low-fat brands)

Frozen juices (such as cranberry, orange, apple)

Low-fat frozen yogurt

Whole-fruit freezer pops

Bakery

Whole-grain breads and rolls

Whole-grain English muffins

Whole-grain pitas

Corn tortillas

Whole wheat or white flour tortillas

Beverages:

Flavored sparkling water

100% fruit juices

Oven-Fried Chicken Chunks with
Peanut Sauce · *Page 37*

Mini Meals and Snacks

1

Spiced-Up Café Latte

PREP TIME: **5 MINUTES** • START TO FINISH: **10 MINUTES** • 4 SERVINGS (¾ CUP EACH) • *Carbohydrate Choices* 0

½ cup ground Italian-roast coffee

1 teaspoon ground nutmeg

½ teaspoon ground allspice

¼ teaspoon ground cinnamon

Dash ground cloves

3 cups water

½ cup vanilla-flavored fat-free soymilk

4 tablespoons reduced-fat whipped cream topping in aerosol can

4 cinnamon sticks (3 inch), if desired

1 In coffee filter or basket of 8- to 12-cup coffeemaker, place ground coffee, nutmeg, allspice, ground cinnamon and cloves. Add 3 cups water to coffeemaker; brew according to manufacturer's directions.

2 In microwavable measuring cup, microwave soymilk uncovered on High about 30 seconds or until warm. Add warmed milk to brewed coffee in coffeepot; stir.

3 Pour into mugs. Top each with 1 tablespoon of the whipped cream topping. Garnish with cinnamon sticks. Serve immediately.

Betty Tip

Make your own version of latte at home and get the heart-health benefits of soymilk at the same time. This spiced-up coffee is very flavorful—you can also use decaf coffee, which is especially nice right before bed.

1 Serving: Calories 25 (Calories from Fat 5); Total Fat 0.5g (Saturated Fat 0g; Trans Fat 0g); Cholesterol 0mg; Sodium 20mg; Total Carbohydrate 4g (Dietary Fiber 0g; Sugars 2g); Protein 0g **% Daily Value:** Vitamin A 0%; Vitamin C 0%; Calcium 4%; Iron 0% **Exchanges:** ½ Other Carbohydrate

Strawberry-Watermelon-Pomegranate Smoothies

PREP TIME: **10 MINUTES** • START TO FINISH: **10 MINUTES** • 5 SERVINGS (1 CUP EACH) • *Carbohydrate Choices*

2 cups frozen whole
strawberries

2 cups diced seeded
watermelon

1 cup pomegranate or
cranberry juice

2 containers (6 oz each)
French vanilla low-fat
yogurt

1 tablespoon honey

1   In blender, place all ingredients.

2   Cover; blend on high speed about 30 seconds or until smooth. Serve immediately.

Betty Tip

This lively combination of fruit is a great pick-me-up first thing in the morning—or anytime. And for just 2 carb choices, you get a healthy dose of vitamin C and calcium.

Be creative and try other combinations of fruit and yogurt, such as raspberries, peaches, pomegranate juice and peach yogurt.

1 Serving: Calories 160 (Calories from Fat 10); Total Fat 1g (Saturated Fat 0.5g; Trans Fat 0g); Cholesterol 0mg; Sodium 50mg; Total Carbohydrate 33g (Dietary Fiber 2g; Sugars 28g); Protein 4g **% Daily Value:** Vitamin A 8%; Vitamin C 70%; Calcium 15%; Iron 6% **Exchanges:** 1 Fruit, ½ Other Carbohydrate, ½ Low-Fat Milk

Raspberry-Banana-Yogurt Smoothies

PREP TIME: **5 MINUTES** • START TO FINISH: **5 MINUTES** • 3 SERVINGS (ABOUT 1 CUP EACH) • *Carbohydrate Choices*

1 container (6 oz) French
   vanilla low-fat yogurt

1½ cups original-flavored
   soymilk

1 cup frozen or fresh
   unsweetened raspberries

1 medium banana, sliced
   (1 cup)

1 In blender or food processor, place all ingredients. Cover; blend on high speed about 30 seconds or until smooth.

2 Pour into 3 glasses. Serve immediately.

Strawberry-Banana-Yogurt Smoothies: Use strawberry yogurt in place of the vanilla yogurt and fresh or frozen strawberries in place of the raspberries.

Betty Tip

For only 2 carb choices, this tasty smoothie contains a bang of nutrition goodness. Yogurt and soymilk team up to give you lots of calcium; raspberries and bananas give you a good amount of fiber and vitamin C.

1 Serving: Calories 190 (Calories from Fat 25); Total Fat 3g (Saturated Fat 1g; Trans Fat 0g); Cholesterol 5mg; Sodium 115mg; Total Carbohydrate 33g (Dietary Fiber 6g; Sugars 21g); Protein 7g **% Daily Value:** Vitamin A 10%; Vitamin C 40%; Calcium 25%; Iron 6% **Exchanges:** ½ Fruit, 1 Other Carbohydrate, 1 Skim Milk

Cheerios®-Yogurt-Fruit Parfaits

PREP TIME: **15 MINUTES** • START TO FINISH: **30 MINUTES** • 4 SERVINGS • *Carbohydrate Choices* 3½

TOPPING

1¼ cups Honey Nut Cheerios®
    cereal

¼ cup old-fashioned or
    quick-cooking oats

¼ cup sweetened dried
    cranberries

¼ cup sliced almonds

2 tablespoons frozen
    (thawed) apple juice
    concentrate

PARFAITS

3 containers (6 oz each)
    strawberry low-fat yogurt

¾ cup sliced fresh
    strawberries

¾ cup fresh blueberries

1 Heat oven to 300°F. Spray 13 × 9-inch pan with cooking spray. In large bowl, stir together topping ingredients. Spread evenly in pan.

2 Bake about 20 minutes or until almonds are lightly browned, stirring halfway through bake time. Cool 5 minutes.

3 For each parfait, in tall narrow glass, place 2 tablespoonfuls yogurt, 1 heaping tablespoon topping and about 2 tablespoons berries. Repeat layers twice. Serve immediately.

Betty Tip

A breakfast in itself, these yummy parfaits are high in fiber, vitamins A and C, calcium and iron. Using cereal in recipes is an easy way to work in whole grains and lots of nutrients—feel free to use your favorite flavor of yogurt and any fruit you fancy.

1 Serving: Calories 300 (Calories from Fat 50); Total Fat 5g (Saturated Fat 1g; Trans Fat 0g); Cholesterol 10mg; Sodium 140mg; Total Carbohydrate 55g (Dietary Fiber 3g; Sugars 37g); Protein 7g **% Daily Value:** Vitamin A 15%; Vitamin C 40%; Calcium 20%; Iron 15% **Exchanges:** 2 Starch, 1 Fruit, ½ Other Carbohydrate, 1 Fat

Pear-Ginger Scones

PREP TIME: **10 MINUTES** • START TO FINISH: **30 MINUTES** • 12 SCONES • *Carbohydrate Choices* 1½

¾ cup Fiber One® cereal

1½ cups all-purpose flour

⅓ cup sugar

2½ teaspoons baking powder

½ teaspoon ground ginger

⅓ cup firm margarine or
butter

½ cup chopped pear

2 egg whites, beaten

4 to 5 tablespoons milk

1 Heat oven to 400°F. Place cereal in resealable food-storage plastic bag; seal bag and crush with rolling pin or meat mallet (or crush in food processor).

2 In medium bowl, stir together flour, sugar, baking powder and ginger; cut in margarine with fork until mixture looks like fine crumbs. Stir in cereal. Stir in pear, egg whites and just enough milk so dough leaves side of bowl.

3 Place dough on lightly floured surface. Knead lightly 10 times. Roll ½ inch thick. Cut dough with 3-inch cutter dipped in flour. (Or roll dough into circle, ½ inch thick, and cut into 12 wedges with knife dipped in flour.) Place about 1 inch apart on ungreased cookie sheet. Brush with milk.

4 Bake about 16 minutes or until golden. Immediately remove from cookie sheet; serve warm.

Betty Tip

Egg whites provide the protein from eggs but don't contain the cholesterol found in egg yolks. That's good news for your heart.

1 Scone: Calories 150 (Calories from Fat 50); Total Fat 5g (Saturated Fat 1g); Cholesterol 0mg; Sodium 190mg; Potassium 70mg; Total Carbohydrate 22g (Dietary Fiber 2g); Protein 2g
% Daily Value: Vitamin A 6%; Vitamin C 0%; Calcium 8%; Iron 10% **Exchanges:** 1 Starch, ½ Other Carbohydrate, 1 Fat

Parmesan–Black Pepper Breadsticks

PREP TIME: **15 MINUTES** • START TO FINISH: **30 MINUTES** • 12 BREADSTICKS • *Carbohydrate Choices* 1

2 cups Bisquick Heart Smart® mix

½ cup plus 1 tablespoon cold water

½ teaspoon cracked black pepper

5 tablespoons shredded Parmesan cheese (about 1¼ oz)

Olive oil cooking spray

Additional cracked black pepper, if desired

1 Heat oven to 400°F. Line cookie sheet with parchment paper to prevent sticking. In medium bowl, stir together Bisquick mix, water, ½ teaspoon pepper and 2 tablespoons of the cheese until soft dough forms.

2 Sprinkle work surface with additional baking mix. Place dough on surface; roll to coat. With rolling pin, roll into 10 × 8-inch rectangle. Spray top of dough with cooking spray. Sprinkle with remaining 3 tablespoons cheese; press in gently. Starting on 10-inch side, cut crosswise into 12 (8-inch) strips. Gently twist each strip. Place ½ inch apart on cookie sheet. Sprinkle with additional pepper.

3 Bake 10 to 12 minutes until light golden brown. Serve warm.

Betty Tip

Try adding a touch of ground red pepper (cayenne) to these cheesy breadsticks. You'll need only about ⅛ teaspoon, unless you really want to spice it up. Just sprinkle the red pepper on with the Parmesan cheese.

1 Breadstick: Calories 90 (Calories from Fat 25); Total Fat 2.5g (Saturated Fat 0.5g; Trans Fat 0g); Cholesterol 0mg; Sodium 260mg; Total Carbohydrate 14g (Dietary Fiber 0g; Sugars 2g); Protein 3g **% Daily Value:** Vitamin A 0%; Vitamin C 0%; Calcium 10%; Iron 4% **Exchanges:** 1 Starch, ½ Fat

Pitas with Hummus-Olive Spread

20 minutes

PREP TIME: **10 MINUTES** • START TO FINISH: **10 MINUTES** • 10 SERVINGS (2 TABLESPOONS SPREAD AND 4 PITA WEDGES EACH) •
Carbohydrate Choices 2

½ can (15 to 16 oz) garbanzo beans, drained, 2 tablespoons liquid reserved

2 tablespoons lemon juice

¼ cup sesame seed

1 small clove garlic, finely chopped

½ teaspoon salt

½ cup pitted kalamata and/ or Spanish olives, chopped, or 1 can (4.25 oz) chopped ripe olives, drained

1 tablespoon Greek vinaigrette or zesty fat-free Italian dressing

7 whole wheat pita breads (6 inch), each cut into 6 wedges

1 In blender or food processor, place garbanzo beans including reserved bean liquid, lemon juice, sesame seed, garlic and salt. Cover; blend on high speed, stopping blender occasionally to scrape sides if necessary, until uniform consistency. Spread mixture on 8- to 10-inch serving plate.

2 In small bowl, mix olives and vinaigrette. Spoon over bean mixture. Serve with pita bread wedges.

Betty Tip

The kalamata olives are very tasty and really make this dip special.

Making a dip, especially a healthy one like this, is great for get-togethers with friends and family.

1 Serving: Calories 180 (Calories from Fat 45); Total Fat 5g (Saturated Fat 0.5g; Trans Fat 0g); Cholesterol 0mg; Sodium 420mg; Total Carbohydrate 27g (Dietary Fiber 4g; Sugars 3g); Protein 6g **% Daily Value:** Vitamin A 0%; Vitamin C 0%; Calcium 2%; Iron 10% **Exchanges:** 1½ Starch, ½ Other Carbohydrate, 1 Fat

Three-Cheese and Bacon Spread

PREP TIME: **15 MINUTES** • START TO FINISH: **15 MINUTES** • 8 SERVINGS (ABOUT 2 TABLESPOONS SPREAD, 2 CRACKERS AND 1 APPLE SLICE EACH) • *Carbohydrate Choices* 1

4 oz (half 8-oz package) fat-free cream cheese, softened

⅓ cup shredded reduced-fat Cheddar cheese

1 tablespoon grated Parmesan cheese

2 tablespoons fat-free (skim) milk

⅛ teaspoon paprika

Dash pepper

¼ cup raisins

2 tablespoons real bacon bits

2 medium green onions, thinly sliced (2 tablespoons)

16 whole-grain crackers

1 large red apple, sliced

1 In small bowl, beat cream cheese, Cheddar cheese, Parmesan cheese, milk, paprika and pepper with electric mixer on medium speed until smooth.

2 Stir in raisins, bacon bits and onions until well blended.

3 Serve spread with crackers and apple slices.

Betty Tip

This sweet and savory spread is terrific on apples, pears, celery or other fruits and vegetables. Look for reduced-fat whole wheat or whole-grain crackers to serve with it.

1 Serving: Calories 100 (Calories from Fat 20); Total Fat 2.5g (Saturated Fat 1g; Trans Fat 0g); Cholesterol 0mg; Sodium 250mg; Total Carbohydrate 15g (Dietary Fiber 1g; Sugars 7g); Protein 5g **% Daily Value:** Vitamin A 4%; Vitamin C 4%; Calcium 8%; Iron 4% **Exchanges:** ½ Starch, ½ Other Carbohydrate, ½ Lean Meat

Caramelized Onion–Shrimp Spread

PREP TIME: **30 MINUTES** • START TO FINISH: **30 MINUTES** • 18 SERVINGS (2 TABLESPOONS SPREAD AND 2 CRACKERS EACH) •
Carbohydrate Choices ½

1 tablespoon butter (do not use margarine)

½ medium onion, thinly sliced (about ½ cup)

1 clove garlic, finely chopped

¼ cup apple jelly

1 container (8 oz) reduced-fat cream cheese, softened

1 bag (4 oz) frozen cooked salad shrimp, thawed, well drained (about 1 cup)

1 teaspoon chopped fresh chives

36 whole-grain crackers

1 In 1-quart saucepan, melt butter over medium-low heat. Add onion; cook 15 minutes, stirring frequently. Add garlic; cook 1 minute, stirring occasionally, until onion and garlic are tender and browned. Stir in apple jelly. Cook, stirring constantly, until melted. Remove from heat. Let stand 5 minutes to cool.

2 Meanwhile, in small bowl, stir together cream cheese and shrimp. On 8-inch plate, spread shrimp mixture into a 5-inch round.

3 Spoon onion mixture over shrimp mixture. Sprinkle with chives. Serve with crackers.

Betty Tip

Think of this easy appetizer to tote to a gathering. Just pack the shrimp mixture, onion mixture and chives in separate containers and take a plate—assemble when you get there.

1 Serving: Calories 80 (Calories from Fat 30); Total Fat 3.5g (Saturated Fat 2g; Trans Fat 0g); Cholesterol 20mg; Sodium 150mg; Total Carbohydrate 10g (Dietary Fiber 0g; Sugars 3g); Protein 3g **% Daily Value:** Vitamin A 4%; Vitamin C 2%; Calcium 2%; Iron 4% **Exchanges:** ½ Starch, 1 Fat

Ginger and Mint Dip with Fruit

PREP TIME: **20 MINUTES** • START TO FINISH: **30 MINUTES** • 6 SERVINGS (2 HEAPING TABLESPOONS DIP AND 2 SKEWERS EACH) •
Carbohydrate Choices **1**

DIP

1¼ cups plain fat-free yogurt

¼ cup packed brown sugar

2 teaspoons chopped fresh
    mint leaves

2 teaspoons grated gingerroot

½ teaspoon grated lemon
    peel

FRUIT SKEWERS

12 bamboo skewers (6 inch)

1 cup fresh raspberries

2 cups melon cubes
    (cantaloupe and/or
    honeydew)

1 In small bowl, mix dip ingredients with wire whisk until smooth. Cover; refrigerate at least 15 minutes to blend flavors.

2 On each skewer, alternately thread 3 raspberries and 2 melon cubes. Serve with dip.

Betty Tip

Increasing the chilling time to 30 minutes or more heightens the flavor of this terrific dip. And if you have any leftovers, it's even more flavorful the next day.

1 Serving: Calories 100 (Calories from Fat 0); Total Fat 0g (Saturated Fat 0g; Trans Fat 0g); Cholesterol 0mg; Sodium 55mg; Total Carbohydrate 20g (Dietary Fiber 2g; Sugars 17g); Protein 4g **% Daily Value:** Vitamin A 20%; Vitamin C 35%; Calcium 10%; Iron 2% **Exchanges:** ½ Fruit, ½ Other Carbohydrate, ½ Skim Milk

Sesame-Feta Veggie Dip

PREP TIME: **15 MINUTES** • START TO FINISH: **30 MINUTES** • 10 SERVINGS (2 HEAPING TABLESPOONS DIP AND 4 VEGETABLE PIECES EACH) • *Carbohydrate Choices* ½

DIP

1 cup reduced-fat cottage
   cheese

¼ cup crumbled reduced-fat
   herb-and-garlic feta cheese

2 tablespoons sesame tahini
   paste (from 1-lb jar)

1 tablespoon coarsely
   chopped fresh Italian
   (flat-leaf) parsley

¼ teaspoon garlic salt

VEGETABLES

¼ lb fresh cauliflower florets
   (2 cups)

¼ lb fresh broccoli florets
   (2 cups)

½ lb fresh asparagus spears,
   trimmed

1 In blender, place dip ingredients. Cover; blend on high speed until smooth. Spoon into small bowl. Cover; refrigerate at least 15 minutes to blend flavors.

2 Meanwhile, in 4-quart Dutch oven, heat 2 quarts water to boiling. Add vegetables; cook about 2 minutes or until crisp-tender. Drain; rinse with cold water. Pat dry.

3 Serve dip with vegetables.

Betty Tip

To save time, serve the dip with veggies that don't need precooking—try carrots, jicama, green or red bell pepper strips, or celery.

The dip keeps well—you can make it a day or two ahead of time, if you like.

1 Serving: Calories 60 (Calories from Fat 20); Total Fat 2.5g (Saturated Fat 0.5g; Trans Fat 0g); Cholesterol 0mg; Sodium 170mg; Total Carbohydrate 5g (Dietary Fiber 2g; Sugars 3g); Protein 6g **% Daily Value:** Vitamin A 8%; Vitamin C 45%; Calcium 6%; Iron 6% **Exchanges:** 1 Vegetable, ½ Medium-Fat Meat

Spicy Cajun Onion Dip

PREP TIME: **15 MINUTES** • START TO FINISH: **30 MINUTES** • 5 SERVINGS (¼ CUP DIP, 4 PEPPER STRIPS, 12 PEA PODS AND 4 SHRIMP EACH) • *Carbohydrate Choices* ½

DIP

¾ cup plain low-fat yogurt

½ cup reduced-fat sour cream

3 medium green onions, chopped (3 tablespoons)

1½ teaspoons Cajun seasoning

2 cloves garlic, finely chopped

VEGETABLES AND SHRIMP

1 medium red bell pepper, cut into 20 strips

½ lb fresh sugar snap pea pods, strings removed

20 cooked deveined peeled large (21 to 30 count) shrimp, thawed if frozen

1   In small bowl, mix dip ingredients with wire whisk until smooth. Cover; refrigerate at least 15 minutes to blend flavors.

2   Serve dip with bell pepper, pea pods and shrimp.

Betty Tip

Low-fat dairy ingredients and seasonings create a flavorful dip; combining it with veggies and shrimp, gives you a nice hit of vitamins, calcium and iron for less than 1 carb choice.

Want extra flavor? Increase the chilling time to 30 minutes.

1 Serving: Calories 110 (Calories from Fat 35); Total Fat 4g (Saturated Fat 2.5g; Trans Fat 0g); Cholesterol 60mg; Sodium 250mg; Total Carbohydrate 9g (Dietary Fiber 2g; Sugars 6g); Protein 9g **% Daily Value:** Vitamin A 30%; Vitamin C 120%; Calcium 15%; Iron 10% **Exchanges:** ½ Other Carbohydrate, 1 Vegetable, 1 Very Lean Meat, ½ Fat

Creamy Cottage Cheese with Cucumbers

(20 minutes)

PREP TIME: **15 MINUTES** • START TO FINISH: **15 MINUTES** • 5 SERVINGS (ABOUT ¼ CUP DIP AND 12 SLICES CUCUMBER EACH) •
Carbohydrate Choices **½**

2 cups 2% reduced-fat cottage cheese

¼ cup reduced-fat sour cream

3 tablespoons chopped fresh chives or green onions

½ teaspoon seasoned salt

¼ teaspoon lemon-pepper seasoning

3 medium cucumbers, cut into ¼-inch slices

1 In medium bowl, mix all ingredients except cucumbers.

2 Serve dip with cucumber slices.

Betty Tip

This satisfying snack has protein and calcium from the cottage cheese, helps you get your veggies, and is low in carbs.

To take it on the go, place a serving of seasoned cottage cheese in a small bowl with a lid and place sliced cucumbers (or vegetables of your choice) in a zipper-topped bag.

1 Serving: Calories 120 (Calories from Fat 30); Total Fat 3.5g (Saturated Fat 2g; Trans Fat 0g); Cholesterol 10mg; Sodium 530mg; Total Carbohydrate 9g (Dietary Fiber 1g; Sugars 6g); Protein 14g
% Daily Value: Vitamin A 6%; Vitamin C 8%; Calcium 10%; Iron 4% **Exchanges:** ½ Other Carbohydrate, 2 Very Lean Meat, ½ Fat

Creamy Apple-Cinnamon Quesadilla

PREP TIME: **15 MINUTES** • START TO FINISH: **20 MINUTES** • 4 SERVINGS (2 WEDGES EACH) • *Carbohydrate Choices* 1/2

1 tablespoon granulated sugar

1/4 teaspoon ground cinnamon

1/4 cup reduced-fat cream cheese (from 8-oz container)

1 tablespoon packed brown sugar

1/4 teaspoon ground cinnamon

2 whole wheat tortillas (8 inch)

1/2 small apple, cut into 1/4-inch slices (1/2 cup)

Cooking spray

1   In small bowl, mix granulated sugar and 1/4 teaspoon cinnamon; set aside. In another small bowl, mix cream cheese, brown sugar and 1/4 teaspoon cinnamon with spoon.

2   Spread cream cheese mixture over tortillas. Place apple slices on cream cheese mixture on 1 tortilla. Top with remaining tortilla, cheese side down. Spray both sides of quesadilla with cooking spray; sprinkle with cinnamon-sugar mixture.

3   Heat 10-inch nonstick skillet over medium heat. Add quesadilla; cook 2 to 3 minutes or until bottom is brown and crisp. Turn quesadilla; cook 2 to 3 minutes longer or until bottom is brown and crisp.

4   Remove quesadilla from skillet to cutting board; let stand 2 to 3 minutes. Cut into 8 wedges to serve.

Betty Tip

This great-tasting little quesadilla is a good one to have the kids help with because it's so easy.

If your family isn't used to whole wheat tortillas, ask them to try something new—they may just like (or love) the new flavor!

1 Serving: Calories 110 (Calories from Fat 25); Total Fat 2.5g (Saturated Fat 1.5g; Trans Fat 0g); Cholesterol 10mg; Sodium 180mg; Total Carbohydrate 18g (Dietary Fiber 2g; Sugars 9g); Protein 3g
% Daily Value: Vitamin A 4%; Vitamin C 0%; Calcium 4%; Iron 4% **Exchanges:** 1 Starch, 1/2 Fat

Cranberry–Chocolate Chex® Snack Mix

PREP TIME: **10 MINUTES** • START TO FINISH: **10 MINUTES** • 24 SERVINGS (½ CUP EACH) • *Carbohydrate Choices* 1

4 cups unsalted unbuttered popped popcorn

2 cups Multi-Bran Chex® cereal

2 cups Chocolate Chex® cereal

1 cup pretzel nuggets or twists

²⁄₃ cup soy nuts (roasted soybeans)

½ cup dark chocolate chips

½ cup sweetened dried cranberries

1 In gallon-size food-storage plastic bag or 3-quart container, mix all ingredients.

2 Seal bag and shake ingredients to mix, or stir ingredients in container. Store tightly covered.

Betty Tip

Vary the ingredients in this easy mix to make it your own—use any combination of cereal, popcorn and nuts. Just keep the proportion of cereal and popcorn high and the chocolate and nuts low.

1 Serving: Calories 80 (Calories from Fat 20); Total Fat 2g (Saturated Fat 1g; Trans Fat 0g); Cholesterol 0mg; Sodium 90mg; Total Carbohydrate 14g (Dietary Fiber 1g; Sugars 6g); Protein 2g **% Daily Value:** Vitamin A 2%; Vitamin C 2%; Calcium 2%; Iron 15% **Exchanges:** 1 Starch

Apple-Honey On-the-Go Bars

PREP TIME: **20 MINUTES** • START TO FINISH: **50 MINUTES** • 16 BARS • *Carbohydrate Choices*

3 cups Fiber One® Honey Clusters® cereal

¼ cup roasted sunflower nuts

⅓ cup honey

¼ cup packed brown sugar

1 cup dried apple slices, coarsely chopped

½ teaspoon ground cinnamon

½ cup peanut butter

1 Butter bottom and sides of 8-inch square pan, or spray with cooking spray. Place cereal in resealable food-storage plastic bag; seal bag and slightly crush with rolling pin or meat mallet (or slightly crush in food processor).

2 In large bowl, mix cereal and sunflower nuts; set aside.

3 In 3-quart saucepan, heat honey, brown sugar, apples and cinnamon just to boiling over medium-high heat, stirring occasionally. Remove from heat; stir in peanut butter. Pour over cereal mixture; stir gently until evenly coated.

4 Press mixture evenly into pan with back of wooden spoon. Refrigerate about 30 minutes or until set. For bars, cut into 4 rows by 4 rows. Store covered at room temperature.

Betty Tip

For a truly on-the-go snack, make these easy bars the night before, toss in a zipper bag and grab them on the way out the door in the morning.

1 Bar: Calories 150 (Calories from Fat 50); Total Fat 5g (Saturated Fat 1g; Trans Fat 0g); Cholesterol 0mg; Sodium 110mg; Total Carbohydrate 23g (Dietary Fiber 3g; Sugars 14g); Protein 3g **% Daily Value:** Vitamin A 0%; Vitamin C 0%; Calcium 2%; Iron 8% **Exchanges:** 1 Starch, ½ Other Carbohydrate, 1 Fat Carbohydrate Choices: 1½

Baked Coconut Shrimp

PREP TIME: **20 MINUTES** • START TO FINISH: **30 MINUTES** • ABOUT 15 SERVINGS (2 SHRIMP AND 2 TEASPOONS SAUCE EACH) •
Carbohydrate Choices 1

¾ cup apricot preserves

2 tablespoons lime juice

½ teaspoon ground mustard

¼ cup all-purpose flour

2 tablespoons packed brown
   sugar

¼ teaspoon salt

Dash ground red pepper
   (cayenne)

1 egg

1 cup shredded coconut

1 lb uncooked deveined
   peeled medium (31 to 35
   count) shrimp, thawed if
   frozen

2 tablespoons butter or
   margarine, melted

1   In 1-quart saucepan, mix apricot preserves, 1 tablespoon of the lime juice and the mustard. Cook over low heat, stirring occasionally, just until preserves are melted. Refrigerate while making shrimp.

2   Move oven rack to lowest position; heat oven to 425°F. Spray rack in broiler pan with cooking spray.

3   In shallow bowl, mix flour, brown sugar, salt and red pepper. In another shallow bowl, beat egg and remaining 1 tablespoon lime juice. In third shallow bowl, place coconut.

4   Coat each shrimp with flour mixture, then dip each side into egg mixture and coat well with coconut. Place on rack in broiler pan. Drizzle with butter.

5   Bake 7 to 8 minutes or until shrimp are pink and firm and coating is beginning to brown. Serve with preserves mixture.

Betty Tip

You can coat the shrimp up to 2 hours ahead of time; drizzle with butter just before baking.

Go ahead, leave the tail shells on so you can pick up the shrimp easily.

1 Serving: Calories 130 (Calories from Fat 40); Total Fat 4.5g (Saturated Fat 3g; Trans Fat 0g); Cholesterol 60mg; Sodium 125mg; Total Carbohydrate 18g (Dietary Fiber 0g; Sugars 12g); Protein 6g **% Daily Value:** Vitamin A 2%; Vitamin C 2%; Calcium 0%; Iron 6% **Exchanges:** 1 Other Carbohydrate, 1 Very Lean Meat, 1 Fat

Oven-Fried Chicken Chunks
with Peanut Sauce

PREP TIME: **10 MINUTES** • START TO FINISH: **30 MINUTES** • 8 SERVINGS • *Carbohydrate Choices* 1

CHICKEN

1½ cups corn flakes cereal, crushed (½ cup)

½ cup Bisquick Heart Smart® mix

¾ teaspoon paprika

¼ teaspoon salt

¼ teaspoon pepper

1 lb boneless skinless chicken breasts, trimmed of fat, cut into 1-inch pieces

Cooking spray

PEANUT SAUCE

½ cup plain fat-free yogurt

¼ cup peanut butter

½ cup fat-free (skim) milk

1 tablespoon soy sauce

⅛ teaspoon ground red pepper (cayenne), if desired

1 Heat oven to 400°F. Line 15 × 10 × 1-inch pan with foil. In 2-quart resealable food-storage plastic bag, mix cereal, Bisquick mix, paprika, salt and pepper. Shake about 6 chicken pieces at a time in bag until coated. Shake off any extra crumbs; place chicken pieces in pan. Spray with cooking spray.

2 Bake uncovered 20 to 25 minutes or until coating is crisp and juice of chicken is clear when center of thickest part is cut (170°F).

3 Meanwhile, in 10-inch nonstick skillet, mix sauce ingredients. Cook over medium heat 3 to 4 minutes, stirring occasionally, until mixture begins to thicken. Serve sauce with chicken.

Betty Tip

Rich in vitamins, minerals and heart-healthy fat, peanut butter helps fill you up and keep you full, and a modest amount may prevent you from overindulging in other foods.

1 Serving: Calories 180 (Calories from Fat 60); Total Fat 6g (Saturated Fat 1.5g; Trans Fat 0g); Cholesterol 35mg; Sodium 390mg; Total Carbohydrate 13g (Dietary Fiber 0g; Sugars 4g); Protein 17g **% Daily Value:** Vitamin A 6%; Vitamin C 0%; Calcium 8%; Iron 15% **Exchanges:** ½ Starch, ½ Other Carbohydrate, 2 Very Lean Meat, 1 Fat

Chipotle Turkey Chili · *Page 44*

Speedy Soups and Sandwiches

2

Italian Chicken Noodle Soup

PREP TIME: **30 MINUTES** • START TO FINISH: **30 MINUTES** • 6 SERVINGS (1½ CUPS EACH) • *Carbohydrate Choices*

1 tablespoon olive or
   canola oil

½ lb boneless skinless
   chicken breasts, cut into
   ½-inch pieces

1 medium onion, chopped
   (½ cup)

2 cans (14 oz each) chicken
   broth

2 cups water

3 medium carrots, sliced
   (1½ cups)

2 cups fresh broccoli florets

1½ cups uncooked medium
   egg noodles

1 teaspoon dried basil leaves

½ teaspoon garlic-pepper
   blend

¼ cup shredded Parmesan
   cheese (1 oz)

1   In 4-quart saucepan, heat oil over medium heat. Add chicken; cook 4 to 6 minutes, stirring occasionally, until no longer pink in center. Stir in onion. Cook 2 to 3 minutes, stirring occasionally, until onion is tender.

2   Stir in broth, water and carrots. Heat to boiling. Cook 5 minutes over medium heat.

3   Stir in broccoli, noodles, basil and garlic-pepper blend. Heat to boiling. Reduce heat; simmer uncovered 8 to 10 minutes, stirring occasionally, until vegetables and noodles are tender. Top each serving with cheese.

Betty Tip

You can substitute boneless skinless chicken thighs for part or all of the chicken breasts—two thighs usually equal one breast.

We used fresh vegetables, but you can use frozen vegetables if it's easier.

1 Serving: Calories 170 (Calories from Fat 60); Total Fat 6g (Saturated Fat 2g; Trans Fat 0g); Cholesterol 35mg; Sodium 730mg; Total Carbohydrate 14g (Dietary Fiber 2g; Sugars 3g); Protein 15g **% Daily Value:** Vitamin A 110%; Vitamin C 25%; Calcium 10%; Iron 8% **Exchanges:** ½ Other Carbohydrate, 1 Vegetable, 2 Very Lean Meat, 1 Fat

Easy Chicken and Bean Stew

PREP TIME: **30 MINUTES** • START TO FINISH: **30 MINUTES** • 4 SERVINGS (1¼ CUPS EACH) • *Carbohydrate Choices* **2½**

1 tablespoon olive or canola oil

1½ cups frozen bell pepper and onion stir-fry (from 1-lb bag)

1½ cups diced cooked chicken

1 can (14.5 oz) Italian-style stewed tomatoes, undrained

1 can (8 oz) tomato sauce

1 can (15 to 16 oz) cannellini beans, drained, rinsed

2 tablespoons chopped fresh basil leaves

1   In 12-inch nonstick skillet, heat oil over medium-high heat. Add stir-fry vegetables; cook 2 to 4 minutes, stirring frequently, until crisp-tender.

2   Stir in chicken, tomatoes, tomato sauce and beans. Heat to boiling. Reduce heat to medium; simmer uncovered 5 to 10 minutes, stirring occasionally and breaking up tomatoes, until thoroughly heated. Sprinkle with basil.

Betty Tip

Red kidney or navy beans are good substitutes for the cannellini beans—use what you have on hand.

1 Serving: Calories 330 (Calories from Fat 70); Total Fat 8g (Saturated Fat 15g; Trans Fat 0g); Cholesterol 45mg; Sodium 640mg; Total Carbohydrate 39g (Dietary Fiber 8g; Sugars 11g); Protein 26g **% Daily Value:** Vitamin A 8%; Vitamin C 25%; Calcium 15%; Iron 30% **Exchanges:** 1 Starch, 1 Other Carbohydrate, 1 Vegetable, 3 Very Lean Meat, 1 Fat

Rio Grande Turkey Soup

PREP TIME: **25 MINUTES** • START TO FINISH: **25 MINUTES** • 6 SERVINGS • *Carbohydrate Choices* **2**

1 can (14 oz) fat-free chicken broth

1 can (28 oz) whole tomatoes, undrained, cut up

1½ cups chunky-style salsa

½ cup water

2 to 3 teaspoons chili powder

1¾ cups frozen southwestern-style corn, black beans, red bell peppers and onions (from 19-oz bag)

1 cup uncooked cavatappi pasta (3 oz)

2 cups cut-up cooked turkey or chicken

¼ cup chopped fresh parsley

1 In 4-quart Dutch oven, heat broth, tomatoes, salsa, water and chili powder to boiling, breaking up tomatoes. Stir in vegetables and pasta. Heat to boiling.

2 Reduce heat; simmer uncovered about 12 minutes, stirring occasionally, until pasta and vegetables are tender. Stir in turkey and parsley; cook until hot.

Betty Tip

Skinless turkey breast is a great choice because it's just about the leanest of all meats—just be sure it's ground breast and not regular ground turkey. For extra flavor, garnish each serving with a dollop of reduced-fat or fat-free sour cream.

1 Serving: Calories 250 (Calories from Fat 70); Total Fat 8g (Saturated Fat 2g; Trans Fat 0g); Cholesterol 50mg; Sodium 930mg; Total Carbohydrate 26g (Dietary Fiber 4g; Sugars 7g); Protein 19g **% Daily Value:** Vitamin A 20%; Vitamin C 20%; Calcium 8%; Iron 20% **Exchanges:** 1 Starch, ½ Other Carbohydrate, 1 Vegetable, 2 Lean Meat

Chipotle Turkey Chili

PREP TIME: **30 MINUTES** • START TO FINISH: **30 MINUTES** • 4 SERVINGS (1¼ CUPS EACH) • *Carbohydrate Choices* 2½

¾ lb lean ground turkey

1 medium onion, chopped
 (½ cup)

1 tablespoon finely chopped
 garlic

1 cup frozen whole kernel
 corn, thawed

1 can (15 oz) cannellini beans,
 undrained

½ cup chicken broth

¼ teaspoon salt

1 chipotle chile in adobo
 sauce (from 7-oz can),
 finely chopped

½ cup reduced-fat sour cream

½ cup chopped fresh cilantro

⅓ cup shredded Colby-
 Monterey Jack cheese
 blend (1⅓ oz)

1   In 4-quart saucepan, cook turkey, onion and garlic over medium-high heat 4 to 6 minutes, stirring occasionally, until turkey is no longer pink; drain.

2   Stir in corn, beans, broth, salt and chile. Heat to boiling. Reduce heat to medium; cover and simmer 10 to 15 minutes to blend flavors, stirring occasionally.

3   Stir in ¼ cup of the sour cream and ¼ cup of the cilantro. Serve with remaining ¼ cup sour cream, ¼ cup cilantro and the cheese.

Betty Tip

Cannellini beans are Italian white kidney beans—red kidney beans or great northern beans can be substituted if you like.

Want a bit more heat? Toss in an additional chopped chipotle chile.

1 Serving: Calories 410 (Calories from Fat 130); Total Fat 14g (Saturated Fat 7g; Trans Fat 0g); Cholesterol 85mg; Sodium 720mg; Total Carbohydrate 37g (Dietary Fiber 7g; Sugars 5g); Protein 33g **% Daily Value:** Vitamin A 10%; Vitamin C 4%; Calcium 20%; Iron 25% **Exchanges:** 2 Starch, ½ Other Carbohydrate, 4 Lean Meat

Creamy Fish and Veggie Chowder

PREP TIME: **15 MINUTES** • START TO FINISH: **30 MINUTES** • 5 SERVINGS (1½ CUPS EACH) • *Carbohydrate Choices* 2

2 teaspoons canola oil

1 small onion, chopped
(¼ cup)

1 medium stalk celery,
chopped (½ cup)

2 cups frozen potatoes
O'Brien with onions and
peppers

1 can (14.75 oz) cream-style
corn

1 can (14 oz) reduced-sodium
chicken broth

½ teaspoon salt

1¼ lb firm white fish fillets
(such as cod or pollock),
skin removed

1 cup fat-free (skim) milk

2 teaspoons cornstarch

1 In 3-quart saucepan, heat oil over medium heat. Add onion and celery; cook 2 to 3 minutes, stirring occasionally, until tender.

2 Stir in potatoes, corn, broth and salt. Heat to boiling. Reduce heat; simmer uncovered about 5 minutes or until potatoes are tender.

3 Add whole fish fillets; cover and cook 5 to 7 minutes or until fish flakes easily with fork. In measuring cup, mix milk and cornstarch; stir into chowder. Heat just to boiling.

Betty Tip

It's best to leave the fish fillets whole when you cook them. Then break the fish up a bit with a fork after cooking—it'll come apart easily.

1 Serving: Calories 260 (Calories from Fat 35); Total Fat 4g (Saturated Fat 0.5g; Trans Fat 0g); Cholesterol 60mg; Sodium 740mg; Total Carbohydrate 28g (Dietary Fiber 2g; Sugars 7g); Protein 27g **% Daily Value:** Vitamin A 4%; Vitamin C 10%; Calcium 10%; Iron 8% **Exchanges:** 2 Starch, 3 Very Lean Meat

Bean and Barley Soup

PREP TIME: **15 MINUTES** • START TO FINISH: **25 MINUTES** • 5 SERVINGS • *Carbohydrate Choices* 5

1 tablespoon canola or soybean oil

2 small onions, sliced

2 cloves garlic, chopped

1 teaspoon ground cumin

½ cup uncooked quick-cooking barley

1 can (15 to 16 oz) garbanzo beans, undrained

1 can (15 oz) black beans, drained, rinsed

1 can (14.5 oz) stewed tomatoes, undrained

1 box (10 oz) frozen lima beans

3 cups water

2 tablespoons chopped fresh cilantro or parsley

1   In 4-quart Dutch oven, heat oil over medium heat. Add onions, garlic and cumin; cook about 3 minutes, stirring occasionally, until onions are crisp-tender.

2   Stir in remaining ingredients except cilantro. Heat to boiling. Reduce heat to low; cover and simmer about 10 minutes or until lima beans are tender. Stir in cilantro.

Betty Tip

Though this recipe appears high in carbohydrates, subtracting the fiber number from the carb number leaves you with only 3½ carbohydrate choices.

1 Serving: Calories 430 (Calories from Fat 50); Total Fat 6g (Saturated Fat 0.5g; Trans Fat 0g); Cholesterol 0mg; Sodium 390mg; Total Carbohydrate 76g (Dietary Fiber 20g; Sugars 7g); Protein 19g **% Daily Value:** Vitamin A 4%; Vitamin C 15%; Calcium 15%; Iron 35% **Exchanges:** 4 Starch, ½ Other Carbohydrate, 1 Vegetable, 1 Very Lean Meat, ½ Fat

Chunky Vegetable Chowder

PREP TIME: **10 MINUTES** • START TO FINISH: **20 MINUTES** • 6 SERVINGS • *Carbohydrate Choices* 3

1 tablespoon butter

1 medium green bell pepper, coarsely chopped (1 cup)

1 medium red bell pepper, coarsely chopped (1 cup)

8 medium green onions, sliced (½ cup)

3 cups water

¾ lb small red potatoes, cut into 1-inch pieces (2½ cups)

1 tablespoon chopped fresh or 1 teaspoon dried thyme leaves

½ teaspoon salt

1 cup fat-free half-and-half

⅛ teaspoon pepper

2 cans (14.75 oz each) cream-style corn

1 In 4-quart Dutch oven, melt butter over medium heat. Add bell peppers and onions; cook 3 minutes, stirring occasionally.

2 Stir in water, potatoes, thyme and salt. Heat to boiling. Reduce heat to low; cover and simmer about 10 minutes or until potatoes are tender.

3 Stir in remaining ingredients; cook about 1 minute or until hot (do not boil).

Betty Tip

Make a meatless meal one or two nights a week. If you're making the switch to meatless eating, you may want to cut your ingredients into larger pieces, as in this hearty chowder, which makes them seem more filling and plentiful.

1 Serving: Calories 240 (Calories from Fat 35); Total Fat 4g (Saturated Fat 2g; Trans Fat 0g); Cholesterol 5mg; Sodium 570mg; Total Carbohydrate 43g (Dietary Fiber 5g; Sugars 9g); Protein 6g
% Daily Value: Vitamin A 20%; Vitamin C 60%; Calcium 8%; Iron 15% **Exchanges:** 2 Starch, ½ Other Carbohydrate, 1 Vegetable, ½ Fat

Savory Millet and Potato Stew

PREP TIME: **30 MINUTES** • START TO FINISH: **30 MINUTES** • 6 SERVINGS (ABOUT 1⅓ CUPS EACH) • *Carbohydrate Choices* 2½

5 cups reduced-sodium chicken broth

2 tablespoons soy sauce

1 bag (1 lb) frozen broccoli, carrots and cauliflower (or other combination)

1 cup diced red potatoes

1 cup uncooked millet

1 teaspoon dried thyme leaves

¼ to ½ teaspoon pepper

1 large onion, chopped (1 cup)

4 cloves garlic, finely chopped

1 In 4-quart saucepan or Dutch oven, heat broth and soy sauce to boiling. Stir in remaining ingredients.

2 Heat to boiling. Reduce heat to medium; cover and cook 12 to 14 minutes, stirring occasionally, until millet and potatoes are tender.

Betty Tip

Whole grains—like millet—are concentrated sources of nutrients and phytochemicals, thought to have health-protective benefits, and they may help control diabetes.

1 Serving: Calories 200 (Calories from Fat 15); Total Fat 15g (Saturated Fat 0g; Trans Fat 0g); Cholesterol 0mg; Sodium 780mg; Total Carbohydrate 37g (Dietary Fiber 6g; Sugars 3g); Protein 9g **% Daily Value:** Vitamin A 30%; Vitamin C 25%; Calcium 6%; Iron 15% **Exchanges:** 2 Starch, 1 Vegetable

Red Pepper–Lentil Soup

PREP TIME: **10 MINUTES** • START TO FINISH: **30 MINUTES** • 4 SERVINGS (1½ CUPS EACH) • *Carbohydrate Choices* **2**

2 teaspoons canola oil

½ cup chopped onion (1 medium)

4 cloves garlic, finely chopped

1 cup dried lentils, sorted, rinsed

1 can (14 oz) fat-free chicken broth with 33% less sodium

3 cups water

4 oz fully cooked low-fat turkey kielbasa, cut lengthwise in half and cut crosswise into slices (1 cup)

½ cup drained roasted red bell peppers, chopped

2 tablespoons chopped fresh basil leaves

⅛ teaspoon pepper

1 In 3-quart saucepan, heat oil over medium-high heat. Add onion and garlic; cook until tender. Stir in lentils, broth and water. Heat to boiling. Reduce heat; cover and simmer 15 minutes.

2 Stir in remaining ingredients. Heat to boiling. Reduce heat; cover and simmer 4 to 5 minutes or until lentils are tender.

Betty Tip

Lentils are great because they not only cook fast, but they're high in fiber, B vitamins and minerals plus low in calories, fat and cholesterol. They also provide protein and complex carbohydrates.

1 Serving: Calories 250 (Calories from Fat 50); Total Fat 6g (Saturated Fat 1g; Trans Fat 0g); Cholesterol 15mg; Sodium 700mg; Total Carbohydrate 32g (Dietary Fiber 8g; Sugars 3g); Protein 17g **% Daily Value:** Vitamin A 30%; Vitamin C 35%; Calcium 4%; Iron 30% **Exchanges:** 2 Starch, 1½ Very Lean Meat, 1 Fat

Grilled Barbecued Beef and Bean Burgers

PREP TIME: **25 MINUTES** • START TO FINISH: **25 MINUTES** • 5 SERVINGS • *Carbohydrate Choices* **3**

½ extra-lean (at least 90%) ground beef

1 can (15 to 16 oz) great northern beans, drained, rinsed

¼ cup finely crushed saltine crackers (about 7 squares)

2 tablespoons barbecue sauce

¼ teaspoon pepper

1 egg

5 teaspoons barbecue sauce

5 whole-grain burger buns, split

Leaf lettuce, sliced tomatoes and sliced onions, if desired

1 Heat gas or charcoal grill. In large bowl, mix beef, beans, cracker crumbs, 2 tablespoons barbecue sauce, the pepper and egg. Shape mixture into 5 patties, about ½ inch thick.

2 Carefully brush canola or soybean oil on grill rack. Place patties on grill over medium heat. Cover grill; cook 5 minutes. Turn patties; spread each patty with 1 teaspoon barbecue sauce. Cook covered 6 to 8 minutes longer or until meat thermometer inserted in center of patties reads 160°F.

3 Place patties in buns with lettuce, tomatoes and onions.

Betty Tip

Have your meat and fiber, too! Mixing ground beef with beans is a great way to enjoy the taste of beef and boost the fiber.

All beans are high in fiber, so next time try using black beans, kidney beans or pinto beans instead of the great northerns.

1 Serving: Calories 320 (Calories from Fat 60); Total Fat 7g (Saturated Fat 25g; Trans Fat 0.5g); Cholesterol 70mg; Sodium 610mg; Total Carbohydrate 43g (Dietary Fiber 7g; Sugars 8g); Protein 21g **% Daily Value:** Vitamin A 0%; Vitamin C 0%; Calcium 10%; Iron 30% **Exchanges:** 2 Starch, 1 Other Carbohydrate, 2 Lean Meat

Asian Turkey Burgers

PREP TIME: **25 MINUTES** • START TO FINISH: **25 MINUTES** • 4 SERVINGS • *Carbohydrate Choices* 1½

1 lb lean ground turkey

¼ cup finely chopped water chestnuts

4 medium green onions, sliced (¼ cup)

2 tablespoons teriyaki marinade and sauce (from 10-oz bottle)

⅛ teaspoon pepper

4 whole wheat hamburger buns

8 slices cucumber or 4 thin slices red bell pepper

4 leaves leaf lettuce

1 Set oven control to broil. In medium bowl, mix turkey, water chestnuts, onions, teriyaki sauce and pepper. Shape mixture into 4 patties, each about ½ inch thick. Place on rack in broiler pan.

2 Broil patties with tops about 6 inches from heat 4 minutes. Turn patties; cook 6 to 8 minutes longer or until meat thermometer inserted in center of patties reads 165°F.

3 Place patties in buns with cucumber slices and lettuce leaves.

Betty Tip

Turkey burgers don't brown as much as beef burgers do—they're done when the centers are no longer pink and the internal temperature is 165°F. If overcooked, they'll become dry.

1 Serving: Calories 290 (Calories from Fat 70); Total Fat 8g (Saturated Fat 2g; Trans Fat 0.5g); Cholesterol 75mg; Sodium 610mg; Total Carbohydrate 23g (Dietary Fiber 3g; Sugars 6g); Protein 30g **% Daily Value:** Vitamin A 4%; Vitamin C 2%; Calcium 6%; Iron 15% **Exchanges:** 1½ Starch, 3½ Very Lean Meat, 1 Fat

Beef and Swiss Sandwiches

PREP TIME: **15 MINUTES** • START TO FINISH: **15 MINUTES** • 4 SERVINGS • *Carbohydrate Choices* 3

⅓ cup chopped sweet onion (such as Bermuda or Maui)

¼ cup (about 12) pimiento-stuffed green olives

1 small clove garlic, peeled

⅛ teaspoon dried oregano leaves

2 teaspoons olive or canola oil

8 slices whole wheat bread

⅓ lb 97% fat-free deli-style thinly sliced roast beef

⅓ lb reduced-fat Swiss cheese (from deli), thinly sliced

1 medium tomato, sliced

1 In food processor, place onion, olives, garlic and oregano. Cover; process with quick on-and-off motions, scraping bowl frequently, until mixture is finely pureed. Add olive oil; process with quick on-and-off motions until well mixed.

2 Spread about 1 tablespoon olive mixture on 1 side of each bread slice. Top 4 slices with roast beef, cheese and tomato. Add remaining bread, olive side down. Cut each sandwich in half.

Betty Tip

Look for low-fat meats and cheeses when purchasing products at the deli—it's an easy way to lower the fat in your everyday meals.

1 Serving: Calories 390 (Calories from Fat 100); Total Fat 11g (Saturated Fat 3g; Trans Fat 0.5g); Cholesterol 35mg; Sodium 760mg; Total Carbohydrate 44g (Dietary Fiber 6g; Sugars 11g); Protein 30g **% Daily Value:** Vitamin A 8%; Vitamin C 8%; Calcium 45%; Iron 20% **Exchanges:** 3 Starch, 3 Very Lean Meat, 1 Fat

Cucumber-Tuna Salad Pitas

PREP TIME: **15 MINUTES** • START TO FINISH: **15 MINUTES** • 4 SERVINGS • *Carbohydrate Choices* 1½

1 pouch (about 7 oz) albacore tuna

¼ cup reduced-fat mayonnaise or salad dressing

¼ cup plain fat-free yogurt

½ cup chopped cucumber

2 tablespoons chopped red onion

2 tablespoons chopped fresh or 1 teaspoon dried dill weed

1 teaspoon salt-free seasoning blend

2 whole wheat pita (pocket) breads (8 inch)

1 cup shredded lettuce

1 small tomato, chopped (½ cup)

1 In medium bowl, mix tuna, reduced-fat mayonnaise, yogurt, cucumber, onion, dill weed and seasoning blend.

2 Cut pita breads in half crosswise to form pockets. Spoon ¼ of mixture into each pita bread half. Add lettuce and tomato.

Betty Tip

You can also spread this mixture on whole wheat tortillas and roll up, if you like.

For a simple cold lunch on a hot summer day, add a piece of fresh fruit and baked chips.

1 Serving: Calories 220 (Calories from Fat 60); Total Fat 7g (Saturated Fat 1g; Trans Fat 0g); Cholesterol 20mg; Sodium 470mg; Total Carbohydrate 23g (Dietary Fiber 3g; Sugars 3g); Protein 18g **% Daily Value:** Vitamin A 8%; Vitamin C 8%; Calcium 6%; Iron 10% **Exchanges:** 1 Starch, ½ Other Carbohydrate, 2 Very Lean Meat, 1 Fat

Salmon Caesar Wraps

20 minutes

PREP TIME: **15 MINUTES** • START TO FINISH: **15 MINUTES** • 2 SERVINGS • *Carbohydrate Choices* 2

1 pouch (7.1 oz) skinless boneless pink salmon

1 cup bite-size pieces romaine lettuce

3 tablespoons fat-free Caesar dressing

2 whole wheat tortillas (8 inch)

4 thin slices tomato

8 thin slices cucumber

1 In medium bowl, mix salmon, lettuce and dressing.

2 Place half of salmon mixture on center of each tortilla. Top with tomato and cucumber. Tightly roll up tortillas.

Betty Tip

Make Tuna Caesar Wraps by using a pouch of tuna instead of the salmon. You can also omit the tortillas and stuff the filling into pita bread halves.

1 Serving: Calories 280 (Calories from Fat 60); Total Fat 6g (Saturated Fat 1g; Trans Fat 0g); Cholesterol 85mg; Sodium 910mg; Total Carbohydrate 29g (Dietary Fiber 5g; Sugars 5g); Protein 27g **% Daily Value:** Vitamin A 35%; Vitamin C 15%; Calcium 30%; Iron 15% **Exchanges:** 2 Starch, 3 Very Lean Meat, ½ Fat

Grilled Fish Tacos

PREP TIME: 20 MINUTES • START TO FINISH: **30 MINUTES** • 4 SERVINGS • *Carbohydrate Choices* 1

2 tablespoons lime juice

2 teaspoons chili powder

1 teaspoon ground cumin

2 tilapia or cod fillets
(5 oz each)

4 whole wheat tortillas
(6 inch)

1 cup shredded lettuce

½ cup black beans (from
15-oz can), drained,
rinsed

¼ cup chopped seeded
tomato

¼ cup shredded reduced-fat
Cheddar cheese (1 oz)

¼ cup reduced-fat sour cream

2 tablespoons chopped fresh
cilantro

1 In resealable freezer plastic bag, mix lime juice, chili powder and cumin. Add fish; seal bag. Turn bag several times to coat fish with marinade. Refrigerate 15 to 20 minutes to marinate.

2 Heat gas or charcoal grill. Carefully brush canola oil on grill rack. Place fish on grill over medium heat. Cover grill; cook 4 to 6 minutes, turning after 2 minutes, until fish flakes easily with fork.

3 Cut fish into bite-size pieces; divide fish among tortillas. Fill with lettuce, beans, tomato, cheese, sour cream and cilantro.

Betty Tip

This is a lighter version of the popular fast-food item, plus the black beans add extra fiber.

If you have leftover beans, just place in a food-storage container and refrigerate. Toss them into soups, salads or casseroles.

1 Serving: Calories 190 (Calories from Fat 40); Total Fat 45g (Saturated Fat 2g; Trans Fat 0g); Cholesterol 45mg; Sodium 250mg; Total Carbohydrate 19g (Dietary Fiber 4g; Sugars 2g); Protein 20g **% Daily Value:** Vitamin A 15%; Vitamin C 4%; Calcium 10%; Iron 10% **Exchanges:** 1 Starch, 2½ Very Lean Meat, ½ Fat

Ultimate California Crab Wraps

PREP TIME: **15 MINUTES** • START TO FINISH: **15 MINUTES** • 4 SANDWICHES • *Carbohydrate Choices* **3**

½ cup (from 8-oz package) ⅓-less-fat cream cheese (Neufchâtel), softened

1½ teaspoons cooked real bacon pieces (from 3-oz jar or package)

1½ teaspoons finely chopped green onion

1½ teaspoons finely chopped carrot

4 reduced-fat flour tortillas (8 inch)

12 spinach leaves

4 roasted red bell peppers (from 7-oz jar), cut in half lengthwise

1 can (6 oz) jumbo lump crabmeat, drained

8 thin slices avocado

1 In small bowl, mix cream cheese, bacon, onion and carrot. Spread 2 tablespoons cream cheese mixture over each tortilla to within 1 inch of edge.

2 Top each tortilla with 3 spinach leaves, 1 roasted pepper strip, 2 tablespoons crabmeat and 2 avocado slices.

3 For each wrap, fold sides of tortilla over filling toward center; fold over ends of tortilla. Cut in half at a diagonal.

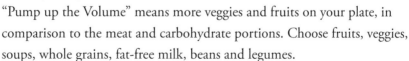

Betty Tip

"Pump up the Volume" means more veggies and fruits on your plate, in comparison to the meat and carbohydrate portions. Choose fruits, veggies, soups, whole grains, fat-free milk, beans and legumes.

1 Sandwich: Calories 350 (Calories from Fat 100); Total Fat 11g (Saturated Fat 5g; Trans Fat 0g); Cholesterol 50mg; Sodium 720mg; Total Carbohydrate 44g (Dietary Fiber 6g; Sugars 8g); Protein 17g **% Daily Value:** Vitamin A 140%; Vitamin C 170%; Calcium 15%; Iron 15% **Exchanges:** 1½ Starch, 1 Other Carbohydrate, 1 Vegetable, 1½ Very Lean Meat, 2 Fat

Lemon-Pepper Walleye Sandwiches

PREP TIME: **15 MINUTES** • START TO FINISH: **15 MINUTES** • 4 SANDWICHES • *Carbohydrate Choices* **1½**

2 tablespoons whole-grain yellow cornmeal

2 tablespoons all-purpose flour

1 teaspoon seasoned salt

½ teaspoon lemon-pepper seasoning

1 tablespoon canola oil

2 walleye fillets (about 6 oz each), each cut crosswise in half

¼ cup tartar sauce

4 whole wheat or rye sandwich buns, toasted

1 cup shredded lettuce

1   In shallow bowl, mix cornmeal, flour, seasoned salt and lemon-pepper seasoning.

2   In 12-inch nonstick skillet, heat oil over medium-high heat. Coat fish fillets with flour mixture; place in skillet. Cook 4 to 6 minutes, turning once, until fish flakes easily with fork.

3   Spread tartar sauce on cut sides of toasted buns. Layer lettuce and fish fillets in buns.

Betty Tip

Walleye is a mild fish—other mild fish such as flounder, cod and tilapia work equally well.

To reduce calories and fat even more, use fat-free tartar sauce.

1 Sandwich: Calories 300 (Calories from Fat 110); Total Fat 13g (Saturated Fat 2g; Trans Fat 0g); Cholesterol 50mg; Sodium 750mg; Total Carbohydrate 25g (Dietary Fiber 3g; Sugars 5g); Protein 21g **% Daily Value:** Vitamin A 4%; Vitamin C 0%; Calcium 4%; Iron 10% **Exchanges:** 1½ Starch, 2½ Very Lean Meat, 2 Fat

Mushroom-Pepper Whole Wheat Sandwiches

PREP TIME: **30 MINUTES** • START TO FINISH: **30 MINUTES** • 4 SANDWICHES • *Carbohydrate Choices* **3**

4 medium fresh portabella mushroom caps (3½ to 4 inch)

4 slices red onion (½ inch thick)

2 tablespoons reduced-fat mayonnaise or salad dressing

2 teaspoons reduced-fat balsamic vinaigrette

8 slices whole wheat bread

4 slices (¾ oz each) reduced-fat mozzarella cheese

8 strips (2 × 1 inch) roasted red bell pepper (from 7-oz jar), patted dry

8 large basil leaves

1 Heat closed medium-size contact grill for 5 minutes.

2 Place mushrooms on grill. Close grill; cook 4 to 5 minutes or until slightly softened. Remove mushrooms from grill. Place onion on grill. Close grill; cook 4 to 5 minutes or until slightly softened. Remove onion from grill.

3 In small bowl, mix mayonnaise and vinaigrette; spread over bread slices. Top 4 bread slices with mushrooms, cheese, onion, bell pepper and basil. Top with remaining bread, mayonnaise sides down.

4 Place 2 sandwiches on grill. Close grill; cook 2 to 3 minutes or until sandwiches are golden brown and toasted. Repeat with remaining 2 sandwiches.

Betty Tip

The whole wheat bread, cheese and portabella mushrooms in these sandwiches make such a great flavor and texture combination, you'll never miss the meat.

1 Sandwich: Calories 340 (Calories from Fat 80); Total Fat 9g (Saturated Fat 25g; Trans Fat 0.5g); Cholesterol 10mg; Sodium 660mg; Total Carbohydrate 50g (Dietary Fiber 7g; Sugars 13g); Protein 16g **% Daily Value:** Vitamin A 10%; Vitamin C 10%; Calcium 25%; Iron 20% **Exchanges:** 2 Starch, 1 Other Carbohydrate, 1 Vegetable, 1 Medium-Fat Meat, ½ Fat

Roasted-Garlic Hummus and Goat Cheese Sandwiches

PREP TIME: **30 MINUTES** • START TO FINISH: **30 MINUTES** • 4 SANDWICHES • *Carbohydrate Choices* 2

1 tablespoon roasted-garlic hummus (from 10-oz container)

1 tablespoon soft goat cheese (from 5.3-oz container)

2 tablespoons chopped pitted kalamata olives

4 small ciabatta rolls (4 inch), cut in half horizontally

3 tablespoons balsamic vinegar

¾ cup sliced peeled cucumber

2 large plum (Roma) tomatoes, cut into thin slices

¼ small red onion, cut into thin slices

½ green bell pepper, cut into thin strips

8 radicchio leaves

1 In small bowl, mix hummus and goat cheese. Stir in olives. Spread 1 teaspoon hummus mixture over cut side of top half of each roll. Brush about 2 teaspoons balsamic vinegar over cut side of bottom half of each roll.

2 On bottom half of each roll, layer 4 cucumber slices, 3 tomato slices, 1 onion slice, 4 bell pepper strips and 2 radicchio leaves. Cover with top halves of rolls. Insert toothpick into each sandwich. Serve immediately.

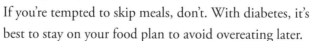

Betty Tip

If you're tempted to skip meals, don't. With diabetes, it's best to stay on your food plan to avoid overeating later.

1 Sandwich: Calories 170 (Calories from Fat 30); Total Fat 35g (Saturated Fat 1g; Trans Fat 0g); Cholesterol 0mg; Sodium 340mg; Total Carbohydrate 29g (Dietary Fiber 2g; Sugars 2g); Protein 6g
% Daily Value: Vitamin A 8%; Vitamin C 30%; Calcium 4%; Iron 10% **Exchanges:** 1½ Starch, 1 Vegetable, ½ Fat

Veggie Burger Packets

PREP TIME: **30 MINUTES** • START TO FINISH: **30 MINUTES** • 4 SERVINGS • *Carbohydrate Choices*

1 cup small whole mushrooms, cut in half

½ medium green bell pepper, cut into bite-size strips

¼ medium red bell pepper, cut into bite-size strips

½ medium red onion, cut into thin wedges

¼ cup honey-mustard barbecue sauce

4 frozen soy-protein burgers

4 whole wheat burger buns, split

1 Heat gas or charcoal grill. Cut 4 (18 x 12-inch) sheets of heavy-duty foil; spray with cooking spray. In large bowl, mix mushrooms, bell pepper strips, onion and barbecue sauce. Place ¼ of vegetable mixture on center of each sheet. Top each with burger.

2 For each packet, bring up 2 sides of foil over burger and vegetables so edges meet. Seal edges, making tight ½-inch fold; fold again, allowing space for heat circulation and expansion. Fold other sides to seal.

3 Place packets, seam side up, on grill over medium heat. Cover grill; cook about 20 minutes, rotating packets ½ turn after 10 minutes, until vegetables are crisp-tender. Remove from grill; let stand 2 minutes. To serve, carefully unfold one end of each packet to center to allow steam to escape. Place burgers and vegetables in buns.

Betty Tip

Serve these easy packets with a crisp green salad and fresh fruit.

If you like, substitute plain barbecue sauce for the honey-mustard flavor.

1 Serving: Calories 260 (Calories from Fat 60); Total Fat 6g (Saturated Fat 15g; Trans Fat 0g); Cholesterol 0mg; Sodium 760mg; Total Carbohydrate 36g (Dietary Fiber 7g; Sugars 11g); Protein 16g **% Daily Value:** Vitamin A 25%; Vitamin C 25%; Calcium 15%; Iron 20% **Exchanges:** 2 Starch, ½ Other Carbohydrate, 1½ Lean Meat

Trail Mix Chicken Salad • *Page 67*

Simple Salads and Vegetables

3

Fajita Salad

PREP TIME: **20 MINUTES** • START TO FINISH: **20 MINUTES** • 4 SERVINGS • *Carbohydrate Choices* ½

¾ lb boneless lean beef sirloin steak

1 tablespoon canola or soybean oil

2 medium bell peppers, cut into strips

1 small onion, thinly sliced

4 cups bite-size pieces salad greens

⅓ cup fat-free Italian dressing

¼ cup plain fat-free yogurt

1 Cut beef across grain into bite-size strips. In 10-inch nonstick skillet, heat oil over medium-high heat. Add beef; cook about 3 minutes, stirring occasionally, until brown. Remove beef from skillet.

2 In same skillet, cook bell peppers and onion about 3 minutes, stirring occasionally, until bell peppers are crisp-tender. Stir in beef.

3 Place salad greens on serving platter. Top with beef mixture. In small bowl, mix dressing and yogurt; drizzle over salad.

Betty Tip

Enjoy this salad—it's an excellent choice as the fat and cholesterol are low, and it's a good source of vitamins and iron with few carbs.

1 Serving: Calories 180 (Calories from Fat 60); Total Fat 7g (Saturated Fat 1.5g; Trans Fat 0g); Cholesterol 50mg; Sodium 270mg; Total Carbohydrate 9g (Dietary Fiber 2g; Sugars 5g); Protein 22g **% Daily Value:** Vitamin A 60%; Vitamin C 100%; Calcium 8%; Iron 15% **Exchanges:** 1 Vegetable, 3 Lean Meat

Trail Mix Chicken Salad

20 minutes

PREP TIME: **15 MINUTES** • START TO FINISH: **15 MINUTES** • 4 SERVINGS (1 CUP EACH) • *Carbohydrate Choices* 1

⅓ cup reduced-fat ranch dressing

2 teaspoons Dijon mustard

1 tablespoon fresh lemon juice

¼ teaspoon dried tarragon leaves

¼ teaspoon dried thyme leaves

3 cups cubed cooked chicken

1 medium stalk celery, sliced (½ cup)

2 medium green onions, chopped (2 tablespoons)

¼ cup dried cherries

¼ cup golden raisins

2 tablespoons sunflower nuts

¼ teaspoon salt

⅛ teaspoon pepper

1 In medium bowl, mix dressing and mustard. Stir in lemon juice, tarragon and thyme.

2 Stir in remaining ingredients. Serve immediately, or refrigerate until chilled.

Betty Tip

Great flavor and crunch, and only 1 carb choice!

Serve this great salad with Parmesan–Black Pepper Breadsticks (page 22), fresh fruit and skim milk.

1 Serving: Calories 320 (Calories from Fat 120); Total Fat 14g (Saturated Fat 2.5g; Trans Fat 0g); Cholesterol 95mg; Sodium 500mg; Total Carbohydrate 19g (Dietary Fiber 2g; Sugars 11g); Protein 31g **% Daily Value:** Vitamin A 8%; Vitamin C 4%; Calcium 6%; Iron 10% **Exchanges:** 1 Other Carbohydrate, 4½ Lean Meat

Chicken, Corn and Avocado Salad

PREP TIME: **30 MINUTES** • START TO FINISH: **30 MINUTES** • 4 SERVINGS (1¼ CUPS EACH) • *Carbohydrate Choices* ❶

1 cup fresh corn kernels (from 2 medium ears)

2 tablespoons reduced-fat mayonnaise or salad dressing

2 tablespoons fat-free sour cream

2 tablespoons lime juice

2 teaspoons 40% less-sodium taco seasoning mix (from 1.25-oz package)

3 cups shredded cooked chicken

1 small red bell pepper, finely chopped (1 cup)

2 medium green onions, finely chopped (2 tablespoons)

½ small avocado, pitted, peeled and cubed (½ cup)

2 tablespoons chopped fresh cilantro

1 In 1-quart saucepan, heat 2 inches of water to boiling. Add corn; reduce heat. Simmer uncovered 5 minutes; drain. Rinse with cold water; drain.

2 In large salad bowl, mix mayonnaise, sour cream, lime juice and seasoning mix with wire whisk. Add chicken, corn, bell pepper and onions; toss to coat.

3 Gently stir in avocado; sprinkle with cilantro.

Betty Tip

Try this salad as a main dish served in lettuce cups or with baked tortilla chips. For a delicious variation, substitute cooked lump crabmeat for the chicken.

1 Serving: Calories 320 (Calories from Fat 130); Total Fat 15g (Saturated Fat 3g; Trans Fat 0g); Cholesterol 95mg; Sodium 240mg; Total Carbohydrate 15g (Dietary Fiber 3g; Sugars 4g); Protein 32g **% Daily Value:** Vitamin A 30%; Vitamin C 130%; Calcium 4%; Iron 10% **Exchanges:** ½ Starch, ½ Other Carbohydrate, 4 Lean Meat, ½ Fat

Sweet-and-Spicy Chicken Salad

20 minutes

PREP TIME: **15 MINUTES** • START TO FINISH: **15 MINUTES** • 4 SERVINGS • *Carbohydrate Choices* 1½

2 teaspoons olive or
   canola oil

1 package (14 oz) uncooked
   chicken breast tenders
   (not breaded)

1 tablespoon jerk seasoning

⅓ cup sweet-and-sour sauce

2 tablespoons packed brown
   sugar

2 tablespoons water

1 tablespoon rice vinegar

1 bag (10 oz) ready-to-eat
   romaine lettuce, chopped
   (about 8 cups)

1 medium green bell pepper,
   chopped (1 cup)

1 can (11 oz) mandarin orange
   segments, drained

1   In 12-inch nonstick skillet, heat oil over medium-high heat. Coat chicken with jerk seasoning; add to skillet. Cook, stirring occasionally, until chicken is no longer pink in center. Remove chicken from skillet; cover to keep warm.

2   In small bowl, mix sweet-and-sour sauce and brown sugar. Add mixture to skillet; cook over medium heat 1 minute, stirring occasionally. Stir in water and vinegar. Stir in lettuce to coat with dressing.

3   Among 4 dinner plates, divide lettuce mixture. Top with chicken, bell pepper and oranges.

Betty Tip

Using chicken breast tenders makes the cooking quick and easy. No preparation is needed, and the chicken breast tenders cook faster than boneless skinless breasts.

1 Serving: Calories 210 (Calories from Fat 30); Total Fat 3.5g (Saturated Fat 0g; Trans Fat 0g); Cholesterol 45mg; Sodium 410mg; Total Carbohydrate 22g (Dietary Fiber 3g; Sugars 17g); Protein 23g **% Daily Value:** Vitamin A 100%; Vitamin C 100%; Calcium 4%; Iron 8% **Exchanges:** ½ Fruit, 1 Other Carbohydrate, 3 Very Lean Meat

Asian Tossed Salad

PREP TIME: **20 MINUTES** • START TO FINISH: **20 MINUTES** • 5 SERVINGS (1 CUP EACH) • *Carbohydrate Choices* **1**

3 cups shredded romaine lettuce

1½ cups (from 16-oz bag) coleslaw mix (shredded cabbage and carrots)

1 cup fresh sugar snap peas, trimmed

½ cup shredded carrots

¼ cup very thinly sliced red onion

¼ cup mayonnaise or salad dressing

¼ cup Chinese chicken salad dressing

1 tablespoon honey

2 tablespoons slivered almonds

1 In large bowl, mix lettuce, coleslaw mix, peas, carrots and onion.

2 In small bowl, mix mayonnaise, salad dressing and honey with wire whisk until smooth. Add dressing mixture to salad; toss to mix. Sprinkle with almonds.

Betty Tip

You can make your own Chinese dressing—just mix ¼ cup reduced-fat mayonnaise, 3 tablespoons citrus vinaigrette dressing, 1 tablespoon soy sauce and 1 tablespoon honey. Toss the dressing with the salad just before serving.

1 Serving: Calories 180 (Calories from Fat 130); Total Fat 14g (Saturated Fat 2g; Trans Fat 0g); Cholesterol 0mg; Sodium 210mg; Total Carbohydrate 11g (Dietary Fiber 2g; Sugars 8g); Protein 2g **% Daily Value:** Vitamin A 90%; Vitamin C 20%; Calcium 4%; Iron 4% **Exchanges:** ½ Other Carbohydrate, 1 Vegetable, 3 Fat

Ahi Tuna Salad with Citrus-Cilantro Vinaigrette

PREP TIME: **30 MINUTES** • START TO FINISH: **30 MINUTES** • 4 SERVINGS • *Carbohydrate Choices* **1**

VINAIGRETTE

1 teaspoon grated orange peel

½ cup fresh orange juice

1 tablespoon chopped fresh cilantro

1 tablespoon lemon juice

1 tablespoon Dijon mustard

1 tablespoon honey

⅛ teaspoon salt

⅛ teaspoon pepper

SALAD

4 sashimi-grade ahi tuna fillets (4 oz each)

1 teaspoon olive oil

½ teaspoon salt

½ teaspoon pepper

6 cups loosely packed mixed salad greens

24 small mandarin orange segments

2 tablespoons chopped green onions (2 medium)

2 teaspoons sliced almonds

1   In small bowl, beat all vinaigrette ingredients with wire whisk until well blended. Cover; refrigerate.

2   Lightly brush both sides of tuna fillets with oil; sprinkle with ½ teaspoon each salt and pepper. In 12-inch nonstick skillet, cook tuna over medium-high heat 1 minute on each side for rare doneness. Place on plate; refrigerate 5 to 10 minutes.

3   On cutting board, cut tuna diagonally into ¼-inch slices.

4   On each of 4 plates, arrange 1½ cups greens; top with 6 orange segments, 1½ teaspoons onions and ½ teaspoon almonds. Arrange tuna on greens. Drizzle 3 tablespoons dressing over tuna and greens on each plate.

Betty Tip

Sashimi-grade tuna is specially processed following Good Manufacturing Processes established by the U.S. government. If sashimi-grade tuna is not available, use regular tuna and cook to an internal temperature of 145°F.

1 Serving: Calories 220 (Calories from Fat 70); Total Fat 8g (Saturated Fat 2g; Trans Fat 0g); Cholesterol 65mg; Sodium 550mg; Total Carbohydrate 14g (Dietary Fiber 3g; Sugars 10g); Protein 24g **% Daily Value:** Vitamin A 100%; Vitamin C 60%; Calcium 6%; Iron 10% **Exchanges:** 1 Other Carbohydrate, 3½ Very Lean Meat, 1 Fat

Cuban-Style Tilapia Salad

PREP TIME: **30 MINUTES** • START TO FINISH: **30 MINUTES** • 4 SERVINGS • *Carbohydrate Choices* **1**

DRESSING

½ cup pineapple juice

1 teaspoon grated lime peel

2 tablespoons lime juice

1 tablespoon canola oil

¼ teaspoon seasoned salt

TILAPIA AND SALAD

4 tilapia or other mild-
flavored fish fillets (about
5 oz each)

Cooking spray

2 tablespoons lime juice

½ teaspoon seasoned salt

4 cups torn mixed salad
greens

2 cups fresh or canned
(drained) pineapple
chunks

¼ cup fresh mint leaves

1   In 1-cup glass measuring cup or small bowl, beat dressing
ingredients with wire whisk.

2   Set oven control to broil. Place fish on rack in broiler pan; spray
tops of fish with cooking spray. Sprinkle tops with 2 tablespoons lime
juice and the seasoned salt. Broil with tops 4 to 6 inches from heat 6 to
8 minutes or until fish flakes easily with fork.

3   Meanwhile, on each of 4 plates, arrange 1 cup salad greens. Divide
pineapple among plates.

4   Place fish on or next to greens. Sprinkle greens and fish with mint.
Serve with dressing.

Betty Tip

For a salad that is heartier and higher in fiber, add 1 cup canned
black beans, drained and rinsed—divide the beans among the plates
with the greens. Serve with whole-grain bread and skim milk.

1 Serving: Calories 240 (Calories from Fat 60); Total Fat 6g (Saturated Fat 0.5g; Trans Fat 0g);
Cholesterol 75mg; Sodium 390mg; Total Carbohydrate 17g (Dietary Fiber 2g; Sugars 11g); Protein 28g
% Daily Value: Vitamin A 60%; Vitamin C 35%; Calcium 6%; Iron 8% **Exchanges:** ½ Fruit, ½ Other
Carbohydrate, 4 Very Lean Meat, 1 Fat

Blueberry and Orange Spinach Salad

PREP TIME: **20 MINUTES** • START TO FINISH: **25 MINUTES** • 5 SERVINGS (1 CUP EACH) • *Carbohydrate Choices* **1**

¼ cup coarsely chopped pecans

2 teaspoons real maple syrup

½ teaspoon sugar

2 tablespoons fresh orange juice

1 tablespoon white wine vinegar

1 tablespoon olive or canola oil

2 teaspoons sugar

4 cups torn fresh spinach leaves

1 cup fresh blueberries

1 medium orange, peeled, separated into segments and segments cut crosswise into thirds

1 Heat oven to 350°F. Line cookie sheet with foil. In small bowl, mix pecans and syrup until pecans are well coated. Spread pecans on foil. Sprinkle with ½ teaspoon sugar. Bake 7 to 9 minutes, stirring occasionally, until pecans are lightly toasted. Cool completely, about 15 minutes.

2 Meanwhile, in small bowl, beat orange juice, vinegar, oil and 2 teaspoons sugar with wire whisk until well blended.

3 In large bowl, toss spinach, blueberries and orange pieces. Pour dressing over salad; toss. Sprinkle with pecans. Serve immediately.

Betty Tip

Blueberries are low-fat and a good source of fiber and vitamin C. Their intense color comes from anthocyanins, potent antioxidants.

1 Serving: Calories 120 (Calories from Fat 60); Total Fat 7g (Saturated Fat 0.5g; Trans Fat 0g); Cholesterol 0mg; Sodium 20mg; Total Carbohydrate 13g (Dietary Fiber 2g; Sugars 10g); Protein 2g **% Daily Value:** Vitamin A 45%; Vitamin C 45%; Calcium 4%; Iron 6% **Exchanges:** ½ Fruit, 1 Vegetable, 1½ Fat

Melon and Grape Salad

PREP TIME: **15 MINUTES** • START TO FINISH: **15 MINUTES** • 4 SERVINGS (½ CUP EACH) • *Carbohydrate Choices* 1

1 tablespoon lemon juice

1 tablespoon honey

1 cup bite-size cubes cantaloupe, honeydew melon or watermelon

1 cup halved red or green grapes

1 teaspoon slivered fresh mint leaves

In medium bowl, mix lemon juice and honey. Add melon and grapes; toss gently to coat. Sprinkle with mint.

1 Serving: Calories 60 (Calories from Fat 0); Total Fat 0g (Saturated Fat 0g; Trans Fat 0g); Cholesterol 0mg;

Betty Tip

For a fancier appearance, use a melon baller to scoop the melon into bite-size rounds.

Sodium 10mg; Total Carbohydrate 15g (Dietary Fiber 0g; Sugars 14g); Protein 0g **% Daily Value:** Vitamin A 30%; Vitamin C 35%; Calcium 0%; Iron 0% **Exchanges:** ½ Fruit, ½ Other Carbohydrate

Roasted Asparagus and Strawberry Salad

PREP TIME: **10 MINUTES** • START TO FINISH: **30 MINUTES** • 4 SERVINGS • *Carbohydrate Choices* ½

1 lb fresh asparagus spears

Cooking spray

4 cups torn mixed salad greens

1 cup sliced fresh strawberries

2 tablespoons chopped pecans

¼ cup balsamic vinaigrette dressing

Cracked black pepper, if desired

1 Heat oven to 400°F. Line 15 × 10 × 1-inch pan with foil; spray with cooking spray. Break off tough ends of asparagus as far down as stalks snap easily. Wash asparagus; cut into 1-inch pieces. Place asparagus in single layer in pan; spray with cooking spray.

2 Bake 10 to 12 minutes or until crisp-tender. Cool completely, about 10 minutes.

3 In medium bowl, mix greens, asparagus, strawberries, pecans and dressing. Sprinkle with pepper.

Betty Tip

Roast the asparagus ahead of time and refrigerate it until you're ready to serve the salad.

Any type of berry works well in place of the strawberries— raspberries, blueberries or blackberries. Just check what's in season at your local farmers' market or grocery store.

1 Serving: Calories 120 (Calories from Fat 70); Total Fat 8g (Saturated Fat 0.5g; Trans Fat 0g); Cholesterol 0mg; Sodium 170mg; Total Carbohydrate 10g (Dietary Fiber 3g; Sugars 6g); Protein 3g **% Daily Value:** Vitamin A 60%; Vitamin C 60%; Calcium 6%; Iron 10% **Exchanges:** ½ Other Carbohydrate, 1 Vegetable, 1½ Fat

Asparagus-Pepper Stir-Fry

PREP TIME: **25 MINUTES** • START TO FINISH: **25 MINUTES** • 4 SERVINGS • *Carbohydrate Choices*

1 lb fresh asparagus spears

1 teaspoon canola oil

1 medium red, yellow or orange bell pepper, cut into ¾-inch pieces

2 cloves garlic, finely chopped

1 tablespoon orange juice

1 tablespoon reduced-sodium soy sauce

½ teaspoon ground ginger

1 Break off tough ends of asparagus as far down as stalks snap easily. Wash asparagus; cut into 1-inch pieces.

2 In 10-inch nonstick skillet or wok, heat oil over medium heat. Add asparagus, bell pepper and garlic; cook 3 to 4 minutes or until crisp-tender, stirring constantly.

3 In small bowl, mix orange juice, soy sauce and ginger until blended; stir into asparagus mixture. Cook and stir 15 to 30 seconds or until vegetables are coated.

Betty Tip

This colorful vegetable stir-fry is high in vitamins A and C, and it's so easy to make.

Bacon and Tomato Frittata (page 112) or Cheesy Steak and Potato Skillet (page 90) would be perfect to serve with this asparagus side dish.

1 Serving: Calories 40 (Calories from Fat 10); Total Fat 1.5g (Saturated Fat 0g; Trans Fat 0g); Cholesterol 0mg; Sodium 135mg; Total Carbohydrate 6g (Dietary Fiber 2g; Sugars 3g); Protein 2g
% Daily Value: Vitamin A 30%; Vitamin C 50%; Calcium 2%; Iron 8% **Exchanges:** 1 Vegetable, ½ Fat

Roasted Sesame Asparagus

20 minutes   **5** ingredients

PREP TIME: **5 MINUTES** • START TO FINISH: **15 MINUTES** • 4 SERVINGS (4 SPEARS EACH) • *Carbohydrate Choices* **0**

1 lb fresh asparagus spears (about 16)

1 tablespoon dark sesame oil

1 teaspoon soy sauce

½ teaspoon wasabi paste

¼ teaspoon black or white sesame seed

1   Heat oven to 450°F. Break off tough ends of asparagus as far down as stalks snap easily. In ungreased 15 × 10 × 1-inch pan, place asparagus spears in single layer.

2   In small bowl, mix remaining ingredients except sesame seed; pour over asparagus, turning asparagus to coat evenly.

3   Roast 8 to 10 minutes or until asparagus is crisp-tender (asparagus will appear slightly charred). Sprinkle with sesame seed.

Betty Tip

Roasting brings out the natural sweetness and flavor of foods. You can roast any vegetable using the directions here—beets, potatoes and garlic are all great when roasted. For roasting times, go to bettycrocker.com.

1 Serving: Calories 50 (Calories from Fat 30); Total Fat 3.5g (Saturated Fat 0.5g; Trans Fat 0g); Cholesterol 0mg; Sodium 75mg; Total Carbohydrate 2g (Dietary Fiber 1g; Sugars 1g); Protein 1g
% Daily Value: Vitamin A 10%; Vitamin C 2%; Calcium 0%; Iron 8% **Exchanges:** ½ Vegetable, 1 Fat

Spicy Green Beans
with Caramelized Onions

PREP TIME: **25 MINUTES** • START TO FINISH: **25 MINUTES** • 8 SERVINGS (½ CUP EACH) • *Carbohydrate Choices*

1 tablespoon olive oil

1 tablespoon sugar

1 large white onion, thinly sliced (1½ cups)

1 lb fresh green beans, trimmed

2 tablespoons reduced-sodium soy sauce

½ teaspoon salt

½ teaspoon crushed red pepper flakes

1 In 10-inch skillet, heat oil and sugar over medium heat, stirring occasionally. Add onion; cook 10 to 15 minutes, stirring frequently, until tender and light golden brown. Remove onion from skillet.

2 To same skillet, add remaining ingredients. Cook 3 to 5 minutes, stirring constantly, until beans are crisp-tender. Stir in onion; cook until thoroughly heated.

Betty Tip

Vegetables fill you up with few calories. That's why the latest American Diabetes Association recommendation is that fruits and vegetables fill half of your plate, meat fill only one-fourth, and a carbohydrate dish fill the remaining fourth. With recipes like this, it's a snap!

1 Serving: Calories 50 (Calories from Fat 15); Total Fat 2g (Saturated Fat 0g; Trans Fat 0g); Cholesterol 0mg; Sodium 280mg; Total Carbohydrate 8g (Dietary Fiber 2g; Sugars 4g); Protein 1g **% Daily Value:** Vitamin A 8%; Vitamin C 4%; Calcium 2%; Iron 2% **Exchanges:** 1 Vegetable, ½ Fat

Broccoli, Pepper and Bacon Toss

20 minutes **5** ingredients

PREP TIME: **15 MINUTES** • START TO FINISH: **15 MINUTES** • 6 SERVINGS (½ CUP EACH) • *Carbohydrate Choices* **1½**

6 cups frozen broccoli florets

2 cups frozen stir-fry bell peppers and onions (from 1-lb bag)

½ cup raisins

2 tablespoons reduced-fat coleslaw dressing

2 tablespoons real bacon pieces (from 2.8-oz package)

1 Cook broccoli and stir-fry bell peppers and onions mixture separately in microwave as directed on packages. Drain well.

2 In large bowl, toss broccoli, bell pepper mixture, raisins and coleslaw dressing. Sprinkle with bacon. Serve warm.

Betty Tip

The small amount of bacon surprisingly adds a lot of flavor to this sweet and savory side dish. It's nice to know you don't have to totally cut out the foods you love, just eat less of them.

1 Serving: Calories 130 (Calories from Fat 20); Total Fat 2g (Saturated Fat 0g; Trans Fat 0g); Cholesterol 0mg; Sodium 70mg; Total Carbohydrate 22g (Dietary Fiber 5g; Sugars 12g); Protein 6g **% Daily Value:** Vitamin A 30%; Vitamin C 60%; Calcium 6%; Iron 6% **Exchanges:** 1 Other Carbohydrate, 1½ Vegetable, ½ Fat

Lemon-Garlic Broccoli with Yellow Peppers

PREP TIME: **20 MINUTES** • START TO FINISH: **20 MINUTES** • 6 SERVINGS (½ CUP EACH) • *Carbohydrate Choices*

4 cups fresh broccoli florets (about 10 oz)

½ cup bite-size strips yellow bell pepper

1 tablespoon olive oil

1 clove garlic, finely chopped

1 tablespoon water

1 teaspoon grated lemon peel

¼ teaspoon salt

1 In 3-quart saucepan, heat 4 cups water to boiling. Add broccoli; heat to boiling. Boil uncovered 2 minutes.

2 Add bell pepper; boil 1 to 2 minutes or until vegetables are crisp-tender. Drain; remove from saucepan.

3 To same saucepan, add oil and garlic. Cook over medium heat, stirring occasionally, until golden. Stir in 1 tablespoon water, the lemon peel and salt. Return broccoli mixture to saucepan; toss to coat.

Betty Tip

Broccoli is a cruciferous vegetable that, like cabbage, Brussels sprouts and cauliflower, is thought to protect against disease, especially certain types of cancer.

1 Serving: Calories 50 (Calories from Fat 20); Total Fat 2.5g (Saturated Fat 0g; Trans Fat 0g); Cholesterol 0mg; Sodium 120mg; Total Carbohydrate 5g (Dietary Fiber 1g; Sugars 1g); Protein 2g
% Daily Value: Vitamin A 8%; Vitamin C 60%; Calcium 4%; Iron 2% **Exchanges:** 1 Vegetable, ½ Fat

Dilly Spinach with Mushrooms

PREP TIME: **15 MINUTES** • START TO FINISH: **15 MINUTES** • 2 SERVINGS (½ CUP EACH) • *Carbohydrate Choices* ½

2 teaspoons olive oil

1 clove garlic, finely chopped

1 cup sliced fresh mushrooms
   (3 oz)

1 bag (6 oz) washed fresh
   baby spinach leaves
   (about 7 cups)

¼ teaspoon salt

⅛ teaspoon dried dill weed

1 tablespoon pine nuts,
   toasted

1 In 4-quart Dutch oven, heat oil over medium heat. Add garlic and mushrooms; cook about 3 minutes, stirring constantly, until mushrooms are crisp-tender.

2 Stir in spinach, salt and dill weed. Cook 3 to 4 minutes, stirring occasionally, until spinach is hot and wilted. Sprinkle with nuts.

Betty Tip

To toast pine nuts, sprinkle in ungreased heavy skillet. Cook over medium heat 5 to 7 minutes, stirring frequently until nuts begin to brown, then stirring constantly until nuts are light brown.

1 Serving: Calories 110 (Calories from Fat 70); Total Fat 8g (Saturated Fat 1g; Trans Fat 0g); Cholesterol 0mg; Sodium 370mg; Total Carbohydrate 6g (Dietary Fiber 3g; Sugars 1g); Protein 4g **% Daily Value:** Vitamin A 160%; Vitamin C 20%; Calcium 8%; Iron 15% **Exchanges:** 1½ Vegetable, 1½ Fat

Better than Mashed Potatoes

PREP TIME: **15 MINUTES** • START TO FINISH: **30 MINUTES** • 5 SERVINGS (½ CUP EACH) • *Carbohydrate Choices*

1 medium head cauliflower
(2 lb), broken into 1-inch
florets

2 cloves garlic, finely chopped

3 tablespoons grated
Parmesan cheese

2 tablespoons reduced-fat
sour cream

1 tablespoon sugar

1 tablespoon butter or
margarine, softened

1 teaspoon chicken bouillon
granules

½ teaspoon salt

⅛ teaspoon pepper

2 tablespoons chopped fresh
chives

1 In 4-quart Dutch oven, heat 1 inch water to boiling. Add cauliflower and garlic; return to boiling. Reduce heat; cover and simmer 10 to 15 minutes or until cauliflower is very soft and tender. Drain well; return to Dutch oven.

2 Stir remaining ingredients into cauliflower. Place cauliflower mixture in food processor. Cover; process until smooth. Garnish with additional chopped fresh chives if desired.

Betty Tip

This mashed cauliflower dish is a great-tasting alternative to mashed potatoes. It goes well with Pecan-Crusted Catfish (page 134) or Apricot-Almond Chicken (page 129).

1 Serving: Calories 90 (Calories from Fat 40); Total Fat 4.5g (Saturated Fat 2.5g; Trans Fat 0g); Cholesterol 10mg; Sodium 520mg; Total Carbohydrate 9g (Dietary Fiber 2g; Sugars 5g); Protein 4g
% Daily Value: Vitamin A 4%; Vitamin C 40%; Calcium 8%; Iron 4% **Exchanges:** ½ Other Carbohydrate, 1 Vegetable, 1 Fat

Roasted Bell Pepper Medley

PREP TIME: **20 MINUTES** • START TO FINISH: **25 MINUTES** • 6 SERVINGS (ABOUT ²/₃ CUP EACH) • *Carbohydrate Choices* ½

1 lb miniature red, yellow or orange bell peppers

6 small Italian pearl onions (cipollini), thinly sliced (½ cup)

2 cloves garlic, finely chopped

1 tablespoon olive oil

½ teaspoon Italian seasoning

1 tablespoon balsamic vinegar

1 teaspoon honey

½ teaspoon Dijon mustard

½ teaspoon salt

Freshly ground black pepper to taste

1 Heat oven to 400°F. Cut bell peppers in half; remove seeds. (For larger peppers, cut lengthwise in half again.)

2 In medium bowl, toss bell peppers, onions, garlic, oil and Italian seasoning. Spoon mixture into 13 × 9-inch pan.

3 Roast 10 to 12 minutes or until bell peppers are crisp-tender.

4 Meanwhile, in small bowl, beat remaining ingredients except ground pepper with wire whisk.

5 Before serving, drizzle oil mixture over bell peppers and onions; sprinkle with ground pepper.

Betty Tip

If you have a hard time finding the pearl onions, use regular green onions.

1 Serving: Calories 50 (Calories from Fat 20); Total Fat 2.5g (Saturated Fat 0g; Trans Fat 0g); Cholesterol 0mg; Sodium 210mg; Total Carbohydrate 6g (Dietary Fiber 1g; Sugars 4g); Protein 0g
% Daily Value: Vitamin A 40%; Vitamin C 100%; Calcium 0%; Iron 2% **Exchanges:** 1 Vegetable, ½ Fat

Bacon and Tomato Frittata • *Page 112*

Fast Skillet Meals

4

Cheesy Steak and Potato Skillet

PREP TIME: **30 MINUTES** • START TO FINISH: **30 MINUTES** • 4 SERVINGS • *Carbohydrate Choices* 2

1 lb boneless beef sirloin steak, cut into 4 serving pieces

½ teaspoon garlic-pepper blend

¼ teaspoon seasoned salt

1 tablespoon canola oil

1½ cups frozen bell pepper and onion stir-fry (from 1-lb bag)

1 bag (1 lb 4 oz) refrigerated home-style potato slices

¾ cup shredded reduced-fat sharp Cheddar cheese (3 oz)

1   Sprinkle beef pieces with ¼ teaspoon of the garlic-pepper blend and ⅛ teaspoon of the seasoned salt. In 12-inch nonstick skillet, cook beef over medium-high heat 3 to 4 minutes, turning once or twice, until brown and desired doneness. Remove from skillet; keep warm.

2   In same skillet, heat oil over medium heat. Add stir-fry vegetables; cook 2 minutes, stirring frequently. Add potatoes; sprinkle with remaining ¼ teaspoon garlic-pepper blend and ⅛ teaspoon seasoned salt. Cook uncovered 8 to 10 minutes, stirring frequently, until tender.

3   Place beef in skillet with potatoes, pushing potatoes around beef. Cook 1 to 2 minutes, turning beef once, until thoroughly heated. Sprinkle with cheese; cover and heat until cheese is melted.

Betty Tip

This easy skillet dish has everything going for it—it's high in calcium and iron and low in carbohydrates. It's also quick to make and kids love it!

To substitute for the frozen bell pepper mixture, use about ¾ cup each of coarsely chopped bell pepper and onion.

1 Serving: Calories 350 (Calories from Fat 80); Total Fat 9g (Saturated Fat 2.5g; Trans Fat 0g); Cholesterol 70mg; Sodium 510mg; Total Carbohydrate 33g (Dietary Fiber 2g; Sugars 3g); Protein 34g **% Daily Value:** Vitamin A 2%; Vitamin C 15%; Calcium 15%; Iron 20% **Exchanges:** 2 Starch, 4 Very Lean Meat, 1 Fat

Quick Taco Skillet Casserole

PREP TIME: **25 MINUTES** • START TO FINISH: **25 MINUTES** • 6 SERVINGS (ABOUT 1^1/$_3$ CUPS EACH) • *Carbohydrate Choices* 3

1 lb extra-lean (at least 90%)
    ground beef

1 medium onion, chopped
    (½ cup)

1½ cups uncooked instant
    brown rice

1 cup chunky-style salsa

1½ cups water

1 can (14.5 to 16 oz) whole
    tomatoes, undrained,
    cut up

1 can (11 oz) whole kernel
    corn with red and green
    peppers, undrained

1 can (6 oz) tomato paste

1 In 12-inch skillet or 4-quart Dutch oven, cook beef and onion over medium-high heat, stirring frequently, until beef is thoroughly cooked; drain well. Return beef mixture to skillet.

2 Stir in remaining ingredients. Heat to boiling over high heat. Reduce heat to medium high; cook 10 to 12 minutes, stirring frequently, until water is absorbed and rice is tender. Stir before serving.

Betty Tip

Kids are sure to love this quick all-family skillet dish. You don't need to tell them how good it is for them and that it's high in vitamins and iron.

1 Serving: Calories 320 (Calories from Fat 70); Total Fat 7g (Saturated Fat 2.5g; Trans Fat 0g); Cholesterol 45mg; Sodium 830mg; Total Carbohydrate 44g (Dietary Fiber 4g; Sugars 10g); Protein 20g **% Daily Value:** Vitamin A 15%; Vitamin C 15%; Calcium 4%; Iron 20% **Exchanges:** 2 Starch, 1 Other Carbohydrate, 2 Lean Meat

Asian Steak Salad

PREP TIME: **20 MINUTES** • START TO FINISH: **20 MINUTES** • 6 SERVINGS • *Carbohydrate Choices* 1

1 lb beef strips for stir-fry

1 package (3 oz) Oriental-flavor ramen noodle soup mix

½ cup Asian marinade and dressing

1 bag (10 oz) romaine and leaf lettuce mix

4 oz fresh snow pea pods (1 cup)

½ cup matchstick-cut carrots (from 10-oz bag)

1 can (11 oz) mandarin orange segments, drained

1 Heat 12-inch nonstick skillet over medium-high heat. Add beef; sprinkle with 1 teaspoon seasoning mix from soup mix. (Discard remaining seasoning mix.) Cook beef 4 to 5 minutes, stirring occasionally, until brown. Stir in 1 tablespoon of the dressing.

2 Break block of noodles from soup mix into small pieces. In large bowl, mix noodles, lettuce, pea pods, carrots and orange segments. Add remaining dressing; toss until well coated.

3 Divide mixture among individual serving plates. Top with beef strips.

Betty Tip

What color is your diet? Even the bright colors of fruits and vegetables tell us that they're good for us. Fruits and veggies contain antioxidants that may help prevent cholesterol from "sticking to" your arteries.

1 Serving: Calories 270 (Calories from Fat 110); Total Fat 12g (Saturated Fat 2.5g; Trans Fat 1g); Cholesterol 45mg; Sodium 310mg; Total Carbohydrate 19g (Dietary Fiber 2g; Sugars 7g); Protein 20g **% Daily Value:** Vitamin A 110%; Vitamin C 50%; Calcium 4%; Iron 15% **Exchanges:** 1 Starch, 1 Vegetable, 2 Lean Meat, 1 Fat

Asian Pork Stir-Fry with Asparagus

PREP TIME: **30 MINUTES** • START TO FINISH: **30 MINUTES** • 4 SERVINGS • *Carbohydrate Choices* 4

2 cups uncooked instant brown rice

2¼ cups water

1 teaspoon olive or canola oil

2 medium green onions, cut into 1-inch pieces (¼ cup)

1 lb boneless center-cut pork loin, cut in half lengthwise, then thinly sliced crosswise

1 lb fresh asparagus spears, cut into 2½-inch pieces

1 medium red bell pepper, cut into 1-inch pieces

3 tablespoons soy sauce

2 tablespoons packed brown sugar

2 tablespoons dry white wine or orange juice

2 teaspoons cornstarch

¾ teaspoon grated gingerroot or ¼ teaspoon ground ginger

1 Cook rice in water as directed on package, omitting butter and salt.

2 Meanwhile, in 12-inch nonstick skillet, heat oil over medium-high heat. Add onions and pork; cook 4 to 6 minutes, turning pork occasionally, until pork is browned. Add asparagus and bell pepper; cook 5 to 7 minutes, stirring occasionally, until asparagus is crisp-tender.

3 In small bowl, mix remaining ingredients, stirring until cornstarch is dissolved.

4 Reduce heat to low. Stir soy sauce mixture into pork mixture; cook until slightly thickened. Serve over rice.

Betty Tip

Using brown rice instead of white rice adds about five times the amount of fiber to your diet because the bran is not milled away during processing—it's a great way to up your daily fiber.

1 Serving: Calories 450 (Calories from Fat 100); Total Fat 12g (Saturated Fat 3.5g; Trans Fat 0g); Cholesterol 70mg; Sodium 750mg; Total Carbohydrate 56g (Dietary Fiber 4g; Sugars 9g); Protein 32g
% Daily Value: Vitamin A 30%; Vitamin C 50%; Calcium 4%; Iron 15% **Exchanges:** 2½ Starch, 1 Other Carbohydrate, 1 Vegetable, 3 Lean Meat

Pork Fajita Wraps

PREP TIME: **20 MINUTES** • START TO FINISH: **30 MINUTES** • 4 WRAPS • *Carbohydrate Choices* **2**

¼ cup lime juice

1½ teaspoons ground cumin

¾ teaspoon salt

4 cloves garlic, finely chopped

½ lb pork tenderloin, cut into very thin slices

1 large onion, thinly sliced

3 medium bell peppers, thinly sliced

4 flour tortillas (8 inch)

1   In shallow glass or plastic dish, mix lime juice, cumin, salt and garlic. Stir in pork. Cover; refrigerate, stirring occasionally, at least 15 minutes but no longer than 24 hours.

2   Remove pork from marinade; reserve marinade. Heat 12-inch nonstick skillet over medium-high heat. Add pork; cook 3 minutes, stirring once. Stir in onion, bell peppers and marinade. Cook 5 to 8 minutes, stirring frequently, until onion and peppers are crisp-tender.

3   For each wrap, place ¼ of pork mixture on center of 1 tortilla. Fold one end of tortilla up about 1 inch over pork mixture; fold right and left sides over folded end, overlapping.

Betty Tip

Try serving these flavorful fajitas with a combination of ½ cup plain yogurt or reduced-fat sour cream and ½ cup salsa—creamy, kicky and good for you!

1 Wrap: Calories 260 (Calories from Fat 60); Total Fat 6g (Saturated Fat 1.5g; Trans Fat 0.5g); Cholesterol 35mg; Sodium 770mg; Total Carbohydrate 34g (Dietary Fiber 3g; Sugars 5g); Protein 18g **% Daily Value:** Vitamin A 6%; Vitamin C 130%; Calcium 10%; Iron 20% **Exchanges:** 2 Starch, 1 Vegetable, 1½ Lean Meat

Lemon Chicken and Tomatoes with Couscous

PREP TIME: **25 MINUTES** • START TO FINISH: **25 MINUTES** • 4 SERVINGS • *Carbohydrate Choices*

4 boneless skinless chicken breasts (about 1¼ lb)

3 tablespoons all-purpose flour

¼ teaspoon pepper

4 teaspoons olive or canola oil

⅔ cup uncooked whole wheat couscous

1 cup water

1 cup fat-free chicken broth with 33% less sodium

2 tablespoons lemon juice

4 very thin slices lemon

2 large tomatoes, thinly sliced

1 Between pieces of plastic wrap or waxed paper, place each chicken breast, smooth side down; gently pound with flat side of meat mallet or rolling pin until about ¼ inch thick.

2 In shallow dish, mix flour and pepper. Coat chicken with flour mixture.

3 In 12-inch nonstick skillet, heat oil over medium-high heat. Add chicken; cook 2 to 3 minutes on each side or until golden brown and no longer pink in center. Remove skillet from heat. Place chicken on plate; cover to keep warm.

4 Cook couscous in water as directed on package.

5 Add broth, lemon juice and lemon slices to same skillet. Heat to boiling over high heat. Cook, stirring constantly, until broth is reduced by half. Return chicken to skillet; cook 1 to 2 minutes to glaze. Remove lemon slices from skillet; discard. Spoon couscous onto serving plates; top with tomato slices. Place chicken over tomato; drizzle with juices in skillet.

Betty Tip

Add some variety—serve this dish with bulgur or quinoa instead of the couscous.

1 Serving: Calories 360 (Calories from Fat 90); Total Fat 10g (Saturated Fat 2g; Trans Fat 0g); Cholesterol 80mg; Sodium 220mg; Total Carbohydrate 33g (Dietary Fiber 4g; Sugars 3g); Protein 35g **% Daily Value:** Vitamin A 15%; Vitamin C 15%; Calcium 4%; Iron 15% **Exchanges:** 2 Starch, 4 Very Lean Meat, 1½ Fat

Curried Turkey Stir-Fry

PREP TIME: **30 MINUTES** • START TO FINISH: **30 MINUTES** • 4 SERVINGS (1¼ CUPS EACH) • *Carbohydrate Choices* **2**

1¼ cups uncooked instant brown rice

2 cups water

¼ teaspoon salt

2 teaspoons canola oil

1 lb turkey breast strips for stir-fry

1 medium red bell pepper, cut into thin strips

2 cups small fresh broccoli florets

1 can (10½ oz) ready-to-serve chicken broth soup

4 teaspoons cornstarch

4 teaspoons curry powder

½ teaspoon ground ginger

¼ teaspoon salt

1   Cook brown rice as directed on package, using water and ¼ teaspoon salt.

2   Meanwhile, in 12-inch nonstick skillet, heat oil over medium-high heat. Add turkey; cook 5 to 8 minutes, stirring frequently, until browned. Stir in bell pepper and broccoli. Cook 2 minutes.

3   In small bowl, mix remaining ingredients. Stir into turkey and vegetables. Heat to boiling. Reduce heat; cover and cook 2 to 3 minutes or until vegetables are crisp-tender and turkey is no longer pink in center. Serve over brown rice.

Betty Tip

If you can't find the ready-to-cook turkey breast strips, you can buy turkey breast tenderloins and cut them into strips.

1 Serving: Calories 320 (Calories from Fat 50); Total Fat 5g (Saturated Fat 0.5g; Trans Fat 0g); Cholesterol 75mg; Sodium 770mg; Total Carbohydrate 35g (Dietary Fiber 4g; Sugars 2g); Protein 33g **% Daily Value:** Vitamin A 25%; Vitamin C 80%; Calcium 6%; Iron 15% **Exchanges:** 2 Starch, 1 Vegetable, 3½ Very Lean Meat, ½ Fat

Halibut and Asparagus Stir-Fry

PREP TIME: **25 MINUTES** • START TO FINISH: **25 MINUTES** • 4 SERVINGS (1^1/$_3$ CUPS EACH) • *Carbohydrate Choices* ½

2 teaspoons olive or
   canola oil

1 lb halibut fillets, cut into
   1-inch pieces

1 medium onion, thinly sliced

3 cloves garlic, finely chopped

1 teaspoon finely chopped
   gingerroot

1 box (9 oz) frozen asparagus
   cuts, thawed, drained

6 ounces whole wheat
   vermicelli or angel hair
   pasta (dry)

1 package (8 oz) sliced fresh
   mushrooms (3 cups)

1 medium tomato, cut into
   thin wedges

2 tablespoons reduced-
   sodium soy sauce

1 tablespoon lemon juice

1 In 12-inch nonstick skillet, heat oil over medium-high heat. Add halibut, onion, garlic, gingerroot and asparagus; cook and stir 2 to 4 minutes or until fish almost flakes with fork. Meanwhile, cook pasta according to package directions, omitting salt.

2 Carefully stir in remaining ingredients. Cook 2 to 3 minutes, stirring frequently, until heated through and fish flakes easily with fork. Serve with pasta and additional reduced-sodium soy sauce if desired.

Betty Tip
When asparagus is in season and plentiful, substitute 1 pound fresh for the frozen.

1 Serving: Calories 170 (Calories from Fat 35); Total Fat 4g (Saturated Fat 0.5g; Trans Fat 0g); Cholesterol 60mg; Sodium 370mg; Total Carbohydrate 9g (Dietary Fiber 2g; Sugars 4g); Protein 26g **% Daily Value:** Vitamin A 15%; Vitamin C 20%; Calcium 4%; Iron 6% **Exchanges:** 1½ Vegetable, 3 Very Lean Meat, ½ Fat

Shrimp and Pepper Stir-Fry

PREP TIME: **30 MINUTES** • START TO FINISH: **30 MINUTES** • 4 SERVINGS (1 CUP STIR-FRY AND ¾ CUP RICE EACH) •
Carbohydrate Choices **2½**

RICE

1½ cups water

1½ cups uncooked instant
  brown rice

GINGER PAN SAUCE

1 tablespoon reduced-sodium
  soy sauce

1 tablespoon water

2 teaspoons cornstarch

¾ teaspoon ground ginger

STIR-FRY

1 tablespoon canola oil

2 medium green onions, finely
  chopped (2 tablespoons)

1 clove garlic, finely chopped

1 medium red bell pepper, cut
  into thin strips (1½ cups)

1 medium green bell pepper,
  cut into thin strips
  (1½ cups)

12 oz uncooked deveined
  peeled medium (31 to
  35 count) shrimp, thawed
  if frozen, tail shells
  removed

1 cup halved cherry tomatoes

1 In 1-quart saucepan, heat 1½ cups water to boiling over high heat. Stir in rice; return to boiling. Reduce heat to low; cover and simmer 5 minutes. Remove from heat. Let stand covered 5 minutes; fluff with fork and let cool slightly.

2 Meanwhile, in small bowl, mix sauce ingredients until smooth; set aside.

3 In 12-inch nonstick skillet, heat oil over medium-high heat. Add onions and garlic; cook 1 minute, stirring frequently. Add bell peppers; cook about 5 minutes, stirring frequently, until softened. Add shrimp and tomatoes; cook 3 to 5 minutes, stirring frequently, until shrimp are pink and peppers are crisp-tender.

4 Stir sauce into shrimp mixture. Heat to boiling; cook and stir until sauce is thickened. Serve over rice.

Betty Tip

Just about any vegetable can stand in for the peppers. If you like, try bite-size pieces of green beans or snow pea pods.

Ice-cold cubed watermelon goes nicely with the stir-fry.

1 Serving: Calories 280 (Calories from Fat 50); Total Fat 5g (Saturated Fat 0g; Trans Fat 0g); Cholesterol 120mg; Sodium 290mg; Total Carbohydrate 39g (Dietary Fiber 3g; Sugars 4g); Protein 17g **% Daily Value:** Vitamin A 35%; Vitamin C 80%; Calcium 4%; Iron 15% **Exchanges:** 1½ Starch, ½ Other Carbohydrate, 1 Vegetable, 1½ Very Lean Meat, 1 Fat

Mediterranean Shrimp with Bulgur

PREP TIME: **25 MINUTES** • START TO FINISH: **25 MINUTES** • 6 SERVINGS (1⅓ CUPS EACH) • *Carbohydrate Choices* **2**

2 cups water

1 cup uncooked bulgur wheat

2 teaspoons olive oil

1 medium onion, chopped
(½ cup)

¼ cup dry white wine or
nonalcoholic wine

2 cans (14.5 oz each) diced
tomatoes with basil,
garlic and oregano,
undrained

3 tablespoons chopped fresh
parsley

1 tablespoon capers, drained

¼ teaspoon freshly ground
black pepper

⅛ teaspoon crushed red
pepper flakes

1 lb uncooked small (36 to
45 count) shrimp, peeled,
deveined

½ cup crumbled reduced-fat
feta cheese (2 oz)

1 In 2-quart saucepan, heat water to boiling. Add bulgur; reduce heat to low. Cover; simmer about 12 minutes or until water is absorbed.

2 Meanwhile, in 12-inch skillet, heat oil over medium heat. Add onion; cook about 4 minutes, stirring occasionally, until tender. Stir in wine; cook 1 minute, stirring frequently.

3 Stir tomatoes, 1½ tablespoons of the parsley, the capers, black pepper and red pepper flakes into onion. Cook 3 minutes. Stir in shrimp. Cover; cook 4 to 5 minutes or until shrimp are pink.

4 Stir cooked bulgur into shrimp mixture. Sprinkle with cheese. Cover; cook 2 minutes. Sprinkle with remaining 1½ tablespoons parsley.

Betty Tip

If you can't find canned tomatoes with basil, garlic and oregano, use plain diced tomatoes and add 1 teaspoon each of finely chopped fresh garlic, dried oregano leaves and dried basil leaves.

1 Serving: Calories 210 (Calories from Fat 35); Total Fat 4g (Saturated Fat 1.5g; Trans Fat 0g); Cholesterol 110mg; Sodium 500mg; Total Carbohydrate 26g (Dietary Fiber 6g; Sugars 5g); Protein 18g
% Daily Value: Vitamin A 10%; Vitamin C 15%; Calcium 10%; Iron 20% **Exchanges:** 1½ Starch, 1 Vegetable, 1½ Very Lean Meat, ½ Fat

Lemon-Basil Shrimp Toss

PREP TIME: **25 MINUTES** • START TO FINISH: **25 MINUTES** • 5 SERVINGS (1½ CUPS EACH) • *Carbohydrate Choices* **3**

8 oz uncooked linguine

2 tablespoons butter or margarine

1 clove garlic, finely chopped

2 cups fresh sugar snap peas, strings removed

1½ cups julienne-cut (matchstick-size) carrots (from 10-oz bag)

1 lb uncooked deveined peeled medium (31 to 35 count) shrimp, thawed if frozen, tail shells removed

1 tablespoon finely chopped fresh or 1 teaspoon dried basil leaves

2 teaspoons grated lemon peel

½ teaspoon salt-free seasoning blend

1 Cook and drain pasta as directed on package, omitting salt.

2 Meanwhile, in 12-inch nonstick skillet, melt 1 tablespoon of the butter over medium-high heat. Add garlic; cook 1 minute, stirring constantly. Add snap peas and carrots; cook 4 to 6 minutes, stirring occasionally, until crisp-tender. Add shrimp; cook 3 to 5 minutes, stirring occasionally, until shrimp are pink.

3 Stir in basil, lemon peel and seasoning blend. Stir in remaining 1 tablespoon butter and pasta. Cook about 1 minute, stirring occasionally, until butter is melted.

Betty Tip
Sugar snap peas have stringy seams that run along the sides. To remove, snap off the tip that is tough and pull the string along each side of the pod.

1 Serving: Calories 330 (Calories from Fat 60); Total Fat 7g (Saturated Fat 3.5g; Trans Fat 0g); Cholesterol 140mg; Sodium 210mg; Total Carbohydrate 45g (Dietary Fiber 4g; Sugars 3g); Protein 22g **% Daily Value:** Vitamin A 130%; Vitamin C 15%; Calcium 6%; Iron 25% **Exchanges:** 2 Starch, ½ Other Carbohydrate, 1 Vegetable, 2 Very Lean Meat, 1 Fat

Salmon-Pasta Toss

PREP TIME: 25 MINUTES • START TO FINISH: **25 MINUTES** • 4 SERVINGS • *Carbohydrate Choices* 4

8 oz uncooked linguine

1 tablespoon olive oil

12 oz skinless salmon fillets, cut into 1-inch pieces

1 cup sliced fresh mushrooms

12 fresh asparagus spears, cut into 1-inch pieces

2 cloves garlic, finely chopped

¼ cup chopped fresh or 2 teaspoons dried basil leaves

12 grape tomatoes

2 medium green onions, sliced (2 tablespoons)

4 teaspoons cornstarch

1 cup chicken broth

¼ cup shredded Parmesan cheese

1 Cook and drain linguine as directed on package, omitting salt.

2 Meanwhile, in 12-inch nonstick skillet, heat oil over medium heat. Add salmon; cook 4 to 5 minutes, stirring gently and frequently, until salmon flakes easily with fork (salmon may break apart). Remove from skillet.

3 Increase heat to medium-high. Add mushrooms, asparagus and garlic to skillet; cook and stir 2 minutes. Stir in basil, tomatoes and onions; cook and stir 1 minute longer.

4 In 2-cup glass measuring cup, stir cornstarch into broth. Add to vegetable mixture; cook and stir 1 to 2 minutes or until sauce is thickened and bubbly. Stir in salmon. Serve over linguine. Sprinkle with cheese.

Betty Tip

Remove the skin before cutting the salmon into pieces. Place the fillet, skin side down, on a cutting board. Using a sharp knife, cut between the flesh and skin, angling the knife down toward the skin and using a sawing motion. Grip the skin tightly with the other hand after a small portion has been removed.

1 Serving: Calories 470 (Calories from Fat 110); Total Fat 12g (Saturated Fat 3.5g; Trans Fat 0g); Cholesterol 60mg; Sodium 430mg; Total Carbohydrate 58g (Dietary Fiber 5g; Sugars 4g); Protein 33g **% Daily Value:** Vitamin A 20%; Vitamin C 10%; Calcium 15%; Iron 25% **Exchanges:** 3 Starch, ½ Other Carbohydrate, 1 Vegetable, 3 Lean Meat

Quinoa Pilaf with Salmon and Asparagus

PREP TIME: **30 MINUTES** • START TO FINISH: **30 MINUTES** • 4 SERVINGS (1¾ CUPS EACH) • *Carbohydrate Choices* 2½

QUINOA

1 cup uncooked quinoa

2 cups water

1 vegetable bouillon cube

SALMON AND ASPARAGUS

4 cups water

1 lb salmon fillets

2 tablespoons butter or margarine

20 fresh asparagus spears, cut diagonally into 2-inch pieces (2 cups)

4 medium green onions, sliced (¼ cup)

1 cup frozen sweet peas, thawed

½ cup halved grape tomatoes

1 teaspoon lemon-pepper seasoning

2 teaspoons chopped fresh or ½ teaspoon dried dill weed

1 Rinse quinoa thoroughly by placing in a fine-mesh strainer and holding under cold running water until water runs clear; drain well.

2 In 2-quart saucepan, heat 2 cups water and the bouillon cube to boiling over high heat. Add quinoa; reduce heat to low. Cover; simmer 10 to 12 minutes or until water is absorbed.

3 Meanwhile, in 12-inch skillet, heat 4 cups water to boiling over high heat. Add salmon, skin side up; reduce heat to low. Cover; simmer 10 to 12 minutes or until fish flakes easily with fork. Remove with slotted spoon to plate; let cool. Discard water. Remove skin from salmon; break into large pieces.

4 Meanwhile, rinse and dry skillet. Melt butter in skillet over medium heat. Add asparagus; cook 5 minutes, stirring frequently. Stir in onions; cook 1 minute, stirring frequently. Stir in peas and tomatoes; cook 1 minute.

5 Gently stir quinoa, salmon, lemon-pepper seasoning and dill weed into asparagus mixture. Cover; cook about 2 minutes or until thoroughly heated.

Betty Tip

Cooking grains in part broth or juice and part water adds extra flavor— a little broth or juice can make a big flavor difference.

1 Serving: Calories 420 (Calories from Fat 130); Total Fat 15g (Saturated Fat 6g; Trans Fat 0g); Cholesterol 90mg; Sodium 520mg; Total Carbohydrate 38g (Dietary Fiber 5g; Sugars 6g); Protein 33g **% Daily Value:** Vitamin A 35%; Vitamin C 10%; Calcium 8%; Iron 40% **Exchanges:** 2 Starch, 1½ Vegetable, 3½ Lean Meat, ½ Fat

Seafood and Vegetables with Rice

PREP TIME: **25 MINUTES** • START TO FINISH: **25 MINUTES** • 6 SERVINGS • *Carbohydrate Choices* 2

1 package (8 oz) sliced fresh
   mushrooms (3 cups)

1 can (14 oz) fat-free chicken
   broth with 33% less
   sodium

3 plum (Roma) tomatoes,
   cut into fourths, sliced
   (1½ cups)

½ cup sliced drained roasted
   red bell peppers (from
   7-oz jar)

½ lb uncooked deveined
   peeled small (36 to 45
   count) shrimp, thawed if
   frozen, tail shells removed

½ lb cod fillets, cubed

6 oz bay scallops

½ cup white wine or chicken
   broth

½ teaspoon salt

¼ to ½ teaspoon red pepper
   sauce

2 cups uncooked instant
   brown rice

¼ cup chopped fresh cilantro

1 In 3-quart saucepan, heat mushrooms and broth to boiling. Stir in remaining ingredients except rice and cilantro. Heat to boiling. Reduce heat; cover and simmer 5 to 7 minutes or until shrimp are pink and firm.

2 Meanwhile, cook rice as directed on package.

3 Stir cilantro into seafood mixture. Serve in bowls over rice.

Betty Tip

Roasted red bell peppers are high in nutrients and fat-free, plus they add a lot of great flavor—and as they come in a jar, they're very convenient to use.

1 Serving: Calories 240 (Calories from Fat 25); Total Fat 2.5g (Saturated Fat 0g; Trans Fat 0g); Cholesterol 80mg; Sodium 370mg; Total Carbohydrate 32g (Dietary Fiber 2g; Sugars 2g); Protein 22g **% Daily Value:** Vitamin A 20%; Vitamin C 20%; Calcium 4%; Iron 10% **Exchanges:** 2 Starch, 2 Very Lean Meat

Mushroom and Spinach Fettuccine

PREP TIME: **30 MINUTES** • START TO FINISH: **30 MINUTES** • 4 SERVINGS (1½ CUPS EACH) • *Carbohydrate Choices* **3**

8 oz uncooked fettuccine

¾ cup roasted garlic-seasoned chicken broth (from 14-oz can)

2 packages (6 oz each) fresh baby button mushrooms, cut in half

6 cups loosely packed fresh spinach, chopped

1 cup cherry tomatoes, cut in half

1½ teaspoons Italian seasoning

½ teaspoon salt

¼ cup evaporated fat-free milk (from 12-oz can)

¼ to ½ cup finely shredded or shaved Parmesan cheese (1 to 2 oz)

1 Cook and drain fettuccine as directed on package, omitting salt.

2 Meanwhile, in 10-inch skillet, heat ¼ cup of the broth to boiling over medium-high heat. Add mushrooms; cook, stirring frequently, until almost all liquid is absorbed. Stir in additional ¼ cup broth. Continue cooking mushrooms 4 to 6 minutes, stirring frequently, until tender.

3 Stir in remaining ¼ cup broth; heat to boiling. Stir in spinach, tomatoes, Italian seasoning and salt. Cook 1 to 2 minutes, stirring constantly, until spinach is wilted. Stir in evaporated milk just until heated through.

4 Place fettuccine on large platter. Top with spinach mixture and cheese.

Betty Tip

Try whole wheat fettuccine for added flavor and texture or mix half whole wheat and half regular pasta.

1 Serving: Calories 290 (Calories from Fat 50); Total Fat 6g (Saturated Fat 2g; Trans Fat 0g); Cholesterol 50mg; Sodium 660mg; Total Carbohydrate 45g (Dietary Fiber 4g; Sugars 4g); Protein 15g **% Daily Value:** Vitamin A 90%; Vitamin C 15%; Calcium 20%; Iron 25% **Exchanges:** 2½ Starch, 2 Vegetable, ½ High-Fat Meat

Szechuan Noodles and Vegetables

PREP TIME: **30 MINUTES** • START TO FINISH: **30 MINUTES** • 4 SERVINGS (2 CUPS EACH) • *Carbohydrate Choices* **3**

1 package (3¾ oz) cellophane noodles (bean threads)

1 tablespoon sesame oil

4 cups chopped bok choy (stems and leaves)

1 cup shredded carrots (about 2 medium)

4 medium green onions, sliced (¼ cup)

1 package (8 oz) sliced fresh mushrooms (3 cups)

2 cups bean sprouts

1 tablespoon chili paste

1 tablespoon soy sauce

¼ teaspoon crushed red pepper flakes

1 can (8 oz) sliced water chestnuts, drained

1 package (12.3 oz) firm tofu, diced

1   In medium bowl, soak noodles in enough water to cover 15 minutes; drain. Cut noodles into 5-inch pieces.

2   Meanwhile, in 12-inch skillet or wok, heat oil over medium-high heat. Add bok choy, carrots, onions and mushrooms; cook about 2 minutes, stirring frequently, until crisp-tender.

3   Stir in noodles and remaining ingredients except tofu. Cook about 3 minutes, stirring occasionally, until hot. Stir in tofu; cook until thoroughly heated.

Betty Tip

This great-tasting stir-fry is worth the effort and with all the veggies and tofu, it's high in nutrients. Just add a glass of skim milk for a complete meal.

1 Serving: Calories 320 (Calories from Fat 70); Total Fat 8g (Saturated Fat 1g; Trans Fat 0g); Cholesterol 0mg; Sodium 490mg; Total Carbohydrate 46g (Dietary Fiber 4g; Sugars 5g); Protein 15g **% Daily Value:** Vitamin A 160%; Vitamin C 40%; Calcium 15%; Iron 15% **Exchanges:** 2 Starch, ½ Other Carbohydrate, 2 Vegetable, ½ Medium-Fat Meat, 1 Fat

Quick Veggie Frittata

20 minutes

PREP TIME: **20 MINUTES** • START TO FINISH: **20 MINUTES** • 4 SERVINGS • *Carbohydrate Choices* 0

4 whole eggs

6 egg whites

¾ teaspoon Italian seasoning

¼ teaspoon salt

Dash pepper

2 teaspoons canola or
    olive oil

2 cups frozen Italian-blend
    vegetables, thawed (from
    1-lb bag)

2 tablespoons shredded
    Parmesan cheese

1 In medium bowl, beat whole eggs, egg whites, Italian seasoning, salt and pepper until well mixed.

2 In 10-inch skillet, heat oil over medium heat. Pour egg mixture into skillet; top with vegetables. Reduce heat to medium-low. Cook 3 to 4 minutes, lifting eggs with spatula to allow uncooked portion to flow to bottom.

3 Cover; cook 7 to 8 minutes longer or until eggs are almost set but top is slightly moist. Top with cheese. Cover; cook 1 to 2 minutes or until cheese is melted.

Betty Tip

You can substitute 2 cups fat-free egg product for the whole eggs and egg whites in this recipe. Also try other frozen vegetable combinations that you like.

1 Serving: Calories 150 (Calories from Fat 80); Total Fat 9g (Saturated Fat 2.5g; Trans Fat 0g); Cholesterol 215mg; Sodium 360mg; Total Carbohydrate 4g (Dietary Fiber 1g; Sugars 2g); Protein 14g
% Daily Value: Vitamin A 20%; Vitamin C 8%; Calcium 10%; Iron 6% **Exchanges:** 1 Vegetable, 1½ Lean Meat, 1 Fat

Italian Frittata with Vinaigrette Tomatoes

PREP TIME: **10 MINUTES** • START TO FINISH: **30 MINUTES** • 6 SERVINGS • *Carbohydrate Choices*

1 can (14 oz) chicken broth

¾ cup uncooked bulgur wheat

1 medium zucchini, sliced, slices cut in half crosswise (1½ cups)

1 cup sliced fresh mushrooms (3 oz)

1 small red bell pepper, chopped (½ cup)

1 small onion, chopped (¼ cup)

½ teaspoon dried oregano leaves

½ teaspoon dried basil leaves

6 eggs

⅓ cup fat-free (skim) milk

¼ teaspoon salt

¼ teaspoon pepper

½ cup shredded mozzarella cheese (2 oz)

3 medium plum (Roma) tomatoes, chopped, drained (1 cup)

2 tablespoons balsamic vinaigrette dressing

1 Heat oven to 350°F. In 12-inch ovenproof nonstick skillet, heat broth to boiling over high heat. Stir in bulgur; reduce heat to low. Top bulgur evenly with zucchini, mushrooms, bell pepper and onion. Sprinkle with oregano and basil. Cover; cook 12 minutes. Fluff bulgur with spatula, mixing with vegetables.

2 Meanwhile, in medium bowl, beat eggs, milk, salt and pepper with wire whisk until well blended.

3 Pour egg mixture evenly over bulgur mixture. Increase heat to medium-low. Cover; cook 5 minutes. Remove cover; sprinkle with cheese. Bake uncovered 5 to 7 minutes or until sharp knife inserted in center of egg mixture comes out clean.

4 Meanwhile, in medium microwavable bowl, mix tomatoes and dressing. Microwave uncovered on High 30 seconds to blend flavors.

5 Cut frittata into wedges (bulgur will form a "crust" on the bottom; use spatula to lift wedge out of skillet). Top with tomato mixture.

Betty Tip

Bulgur wheat adds an extra chewiness and heartiness to this fantastic frittata, and kids love it!

One teaspoon Italian seasoning is an easy substitute for the oregano and basil.

1 Serving: Calories 230 (Calories from Fat 90); Total Fat 10g (Saturated Fat 3.5g; Trans Fat 0g); Cholesterol 215mg; Sodium 560mg; Total Carbohydrate 20g (Dietary Fiber 4g; Sugars 4g); Protein 14g **% Daily Value:** Vitamin A 20%; Vitamin C 30%; Calcium 15%; Iron 10% **Exchanges:** 1 Other Carbohydrate, 1 Vegetable, 1½ Very Lean Meat, 2 Fat

Bacon and Tomato Frittata

20 minutes

PREP TIME: **20 MINUTES** • START TO FINISH: **20 MINUTES** • 4 SERVINGS • *Carbohydrate Choices* 0

1 carton (16 oz) fat-free egg product or 8 eggs

¼ teaspoon salt-free garlic-and-herb seasoning

¼ teaspoon salt

1 tablespoon canola or soybean oil

4 medium green onions, sliced (¼ cup)

2 large plum (Roma) tomatoes, sliced

½ cup shredded sharp Cheddar cheese (2 oz)

2 tablespoons real bacon pieces (from 2.8-oz package)

2 tablespoons reduced-fat sour cream

1 In medium bowl, mix egg product, garlic-and-herb seasoning and salt; set aside.

2 In 10-inch nonstick ovenproof skillet, heat oil over medium heat. Add onions; cook and stir 1 minute. Reduce heat to medium-low. Pour egg mixture into skillet. Cook 6 to 9 minutes, gently lifting edges of cooked portions with spatula so that uncooked egg mixture can flow to bottom of skillet, until set.

3 Set oven control to broil. Top frittata with tomatoes, cheese and bacon. Broil with top 4 inches from heat 1 to 2 minutes or until cheese is melted. Top each serving with sour cream.

Betty Tip

In recipes that call for whole eggs, you can use either real eggs or egg substitute. Rest assured that the recipe works well either way.

Eggs are full of nutrients—the key is not to have more than three or four a week since they're high in cholesterol.

1 Serving: Calories 180 (Calories from Fat 90); Total Fat 10g (Saturated Fat 4g; Trans Fat 0g); Cholesterol 20mg; Sodium 570mg; Total Carbohydrate 4g (Dietary Fiber 1g; Sugars 2g); Protein 18g **% Daily Value:** Vitamin A 20%; Vitamin C 4%; Calcium 15%; Iron 15% **Exchanges:** 2½ Very Lean Meat, 2 Fat

Southwestern Frittata

PREP TIME: **15 MINUTES** • START TO FINISH: **25 MINUTES** • 4 SERVINGS • *Carbohydrate Choices*

8 eggs

¼ cup water

½ teaspoon salt

½ teaspoon ground cumin

¼ teaspoon coarse ground black pepper

⅔ cup chopped red bell pepper

⅔ cup frozen whole kernel corn, thawed

3 tablespoons chopped fresh cilantro or parsley

2 tablespoons chopped onion

½ cup shredded taco-seasoned cheese blend (2 oz)

1 Heat oven to 350°F. In medium bowl, beat eggs, water, salt, cumin and pepper with wire whisk until blended. In small bowl, mix remaining ingredients except cheese.

2 Spray 10-inch ovenproof skillet with cooking spray; heat over medium-high heat. Pour egg mixture into hot skillet. Reduce heat to medium; spoon vegetable mixture over egg mixture. Cook 5 minutes, lifting edges occasionally and tipping skillet to allow uncooked egg mixture to flow to bottom of skillet. Sprinkle with cheese.

3 Place skillet in oven; bake 9 to 10 minutes or until eggs are set. Cut into wedges to serve.

Betty Tip

Reduced-fat shredded Cheddar cheese can be substituted for the taco-seasoned cheese blend.

Serve this low-carb, high-nutrient frittata with a slice of toast, fresh fruit and a glass of skim milk.

1 Serving: Calories 240 (Calories from Fat 140); Total Fat 15g (Saturated Fat 6g; Trans Fat 0g); Cholesterol 435mg; Sodium 820mg; Total Carbohydrate 9g (Dietary Fiber 1g; Sugars 4g); Protein 17g **% Daily Value:** Vitamin A 35%; Vitamin C 40%; Calcium 15%; Iron 10% **Exchanges:** ½ Other Carbohydrate, 2½ Medium-Fat Meat, ½ Fat

Lime- and Chili-Rubbed
Chicken Breasts
• *Page 128*

Meat, Poultry and Fish

5

Simple Teriyaki Steak Dinner

PREP TIME: 20 MINUTES • **START TO FINISH: 20 MINUTES** • 4 SERVINGS • *Carbohydrate Choices* ½

1 tablespoon butter or margarine

1 medium bell pepper (any color), coarsely chopped (1 cup)

1½ cups sliced fresh mushrooms (about 5 oz)

4 boneless beef top loin steaks (New York, Kansas City or strip steaks), about ¾ inch thick (6 oz each)

½ teaspoon garlic salt

¼ teaspoon coarse ground black pepper

¼ cup teriyaki baste and glaze (from 12-oz bottle)

2 tablespoons water

1   In 12-inch nonstick skillet, melt butter over medium-high heat. Add bell pepper; cook 2 minutes, stirring frequently. Stir in mushrooms. Cook 2 to 3 minutes, stirring frequently, until vegetables are tender. Remove vegetable mixture from skillet; cover to keep warm.

2   Sprinkle beef steaks with garlic salt and pepper. In same skillet, cook steaks over medium heat 6 to 8 minutes, turning once or twice, until desired doneness.

3   Return vegetables to skillet. Stir teriyaki glaze and water into vegetables and spoon over steaks. Cook about 1 minute, stirring vegetables occasionally, until thoroughly heated.

Betty Tip

Mix up some roasted garlic mashed potatoes to serve with the steaks, or surprise your family with Better Than Mashed Potatoes (page 86).

1 Serving: Calories 330 (Calories from Fat 130); Total Fat 15g (Saturated Fat 6g; Trans Fat 0.5g); Cholesterol 80mg; Sodium 600mg; Total Carbohydrate 8g (Dietary Fiber 0g; Sugars 6g); Protein 41g **% Daily Value:** Vitamin A 4%; Vitamin C 20%; Calcium 4%; Iron 25% **Exchanges:** ½ Other Carbohydrate, 5½ Lean Meat

Steak Marsala

PREP TIME: **20 MINUTES** • START TO FINISH: **20 MINUTES** • 4 SERVINGS • *Carbohydrate Choices* 0

4 beef tenderloin steaks, ¾ inch thick (about 1 lb)

½ teaspoon salt

¼ teaspoon pepper

2 cloves garlic, crushed

1 tablespoon drained capers

½ cup Marsala wine or nonalcoholic red wine

1 Sprinkle both sides of each beef steak with salt and pepper. Rub with garlic. Spray 10-inch skillet with cooking spray; heat over medium-high heat. Add beef; cook 6 to 8 minutes, turning once, until desired doneness. Remove beef from skillet; cover to keep warm.

2 Add capers and wine to skillet. Heat to boiling over high heat. Cook uncovered 3 to 4 minutes, stirring frequently, until liquid is slightly reduced. Serve sauce over beef.

Betty Tip

You can enjoy red meat in moderation as it contains protein and iron.

Curried Coconut Couscous (page 156) and Asparagus-Pepper Stir-Fry (page 78) are great to serve with these steaks.

1 Serving: Calories 190 (Calories from Fat 70); Total Fat 8g (Saturated Fat 3g; Trans Fat 0g); Cholesterol 50mg; Sodium 390mg; Total Carbohydrate 2g (Dietary Fiber 0g; Sugars 0g); Protein 26g **% Daily Value:** Vitamin A 0%; Vitamin C 0%; Calcium 0%; Iron 15% **Exchanges:** 3½ Lean Meat

Szechuan Beef and Bean Sprouts

PREP TIME: **20 MINUTES** • START TO FINISH: **30 MINUTES** • 4 SERVINGS (1¼ CUPS EACH) • *Carbohydrate Choices* ½

1 lb boneless beef eye of
round steak, trimmed
of fat

¼ cup fat-free chicken broth
with 33% less sodium

1 tablespoon soy sauce

1 tablespoon Szechuan
(Sichuan or Szechwan)
sauce

⅛ teaspoon crushed red
pepper flakes

4 plum (Roma) tomatoes, cut
into eighths

2 cups fresh bean sprouts
(4 oz)

1 tablespoon chopped fresh
cilantro

1   Cut beef with grain into 2-inch strips; cut strips across grain into ⅛-inch slices. (Beef is easier to cut if partially frozen, 30 to 60 minutes.) In medium bowl, mix broth, soy sauce, Szechuan sauce and red pepper. Stir in beef. Let stand 10 minutes.

2   Drain beef; reserve marinade. Heat 12-inch nonstick skillet over medium-high heat. Add half of the beef to skillet; cook and stir 2 to 3 minutes or until brown. Remove beef from skillet. Repeat with remaining beef. Return all beef to skillet.

3   Add reserved marinade, the tomatoes and bean sprouts to beef in skillet; cook and stir about 1 minute or until vegetables are warm. Sprinkle with cilantro.

Betty Tip

Using a nonstick skillet keeps the food from sticking, and eliminates the fat that most traditional stir-fries use.

If fresh bean sprouts are not available, it's okay to substitute a 14-ounce can of bean sprouts. Just be sure to drain and rinse them so they seem more like fresh ones.

1 Serving: Calories 200 (Calories from Fat 50); Total Fat 6g (Saturated Fat 1.5g; Trans Fat 0g); Cholesterol 65mg; Sodium 430mg; Total Carbohydrate 6g (Dietary Fiber 1g; Sugars 3g); Protein 30g **% Daily Value:** Vitamin A 10%; Vitamin C 20%; Calcium 2%; Iron 20% **Exchanges:** 1 Vegetable, 4 Very Lean Meat, 1 Fat

Latin-Style Flank Steak with Spicy Parsley Pesto

PREP TIME: **20 MINUTES** • START TO FINISH: **20 MINUTES** • 4 SERVINGS • *Carbohydrate Choices* 0

STEAK

1 lb beef flank steak

¼ teaspoon pepper

⅛ teaspoon salt

PESTO

½ cup chopped fresh flat-leaf
  or curly-leaf parsley

2 teaspoons red wine vinegar

5 or 6 drops red pepper sauce

⅛ teaspoon salt

⅛ teaspoon ground cumin

1   Set oven control to broil. Place beef on rack in broiler pan. Sprinkle with pepper and ⅛ teaspoon salt. Broil with top 4 to 6 inches from heat 10 to 12 minutes, turning once, until desired doneness.

2   Meanwhile, in small bowl, mix pesto ingredients.

3   Cut beef across grain into thin strips. Serve beef with pesto.

Betty Tip

Spices and herbs boost the flavor of these yummy steaks. And the best part? This pesto has fewer calories and less fat than regular pesto.

1 Serving: Calories 180 (Calories from Fat 70); Total Fat 8g (Saturated Fat 3g; Trans Fat 0g); Cholesterol 50mg; Sodium 190mg; Total Carbohydrate 0g (Dietary Fiber 0g; Sugars 0g); Protein 26g **% Daily Value:** Vitamin A 15%; Vitamin C 8%; Calcium 0%; Iron 15% **Exchanges:** 3½ Lean Meat

Pork with Caramelized Onions

PREP TIME: **15 MINUTES** • START TO FINISH: **25 MINUTES** • 4 SERVINGS • *Carbohydrate Choices* ½

1 lb pork tenderloin

½ teaspoon salt

¼ teaspoon paprika

1 large onion, thinly sliced
  (2 cups)

¼ teaspoon sugar

1 Cut pork into ½-inch slices. Sprinkle both sides of pork with salt and paprika.

2 Heat 10-inch nonstick skillet over medium-high heat. Add pork; cook 6 to 8 minutes, turning once, until no longer pink in center. Remove pork from skillet; keep warm. Wipe out skillet.

3 Heat same skillet over medium-high heat. Add onion; cook 1 minute, stirring frequently. Reduce heat to medium. Stir in sugar. Cook about 3 minutes longer, stirring frequently, until onion is soft and golden brown. Spoon over pork.

Betty Tip

Check to be certain that the meat you purchase is pork tenderloin, not pork loin. Tenderloin is more tender than loin and is lower in fat.

1 Serving: Calories 170 (Calories from Fat 40); Total Fat 4.5g (Saturated Fat 1.5g; Trans Fat 0g); Cholesterol 70mg; Sodium 350mg; Total Carbohydrate 6g (Dietary Fiber 1g; Sugars 3g); Protein 26g **% Daily Value:** Vitamin A 0%; Vitamin C 4%; Calcium 0%; Iron 8% **Exchanges:** 1 Vegetable, 3½ Very Lean Meat, ½ Fat

Peppered Pork Medallions in Tangy Mushroom Sauce

PREP TIME: **30 MINUTES** • START TO FINISH: **30 MINUTES** • 4 SERVINGS • *Carbohydrate Choices*

1 lb pork tenderloin

1 teaspoon seasoned pepper blend

¼ teaspoon salt

2 teaspoons canola oil

1 cup fat-free chicken broth with 33% less sodium

2 tablespoons all-purpose flour

2 tablespoons balsamic vinegar

2 teaspoons dried rosemary leaves, crumbled

1 package (8 oz) fresh whole mushrooms

1 Cut pork into 4 serving pieces. Between sheets of plastic wrap or waxed paper, flatten pork pieces with meat mallet to 4 × 3½ inches and less than ½ inch thick.

2 Sprinkle both sides of pork medallions with pepper blend and salt; press in seasonings. In 12-inch nonstick skillet, heat oil over medium-high heat. Add pork; cook about 5 minutes, turning once, until browned.

3 Meanwhile, in small bowl, mix broth and flour until smooth. Add broth mixture and remaining ingredients to skillet. Heat to boiling. Reduce heat; cover and cook 8 to 10 minutes, stirring occasionally, until pork is no longer pink in center and mushrooms are tender.

Betty Tip

You can try thyme, oregano or parsley instead of the rosemary.

Small crimini mushrooms have a slightly more earthy flavor and meatier texture if you'd like to substitute them for the regular white mushrooms.

1 Serving: Calories 200 (Calories from Fat 60); Total Fat 7g (Saturated Fat 2g; Trans Fat 0g); Cholesterol 70mg; Sodium 340mg; Total Carbohydrate 6g (Dietary Fiber 1g; Sugars 1g); Protein 29g
% Daily Value: Vitamin A 0%; Vitamin C 0%; Calcium 2%; Iron 15% **Exchanges:** ½ Other Carbohydrate, 4 Very Lean Meat, 1 Fat

Pork Lo Mein

PREP TIME: **25 MINUTES** • START TO FINISH: **25 MINUTES** • 4 SERVINGS • *Carbohydrate Choices* **2**

½ lb boneless pork loin

2½ cups fresh sugar snap peas

1½ cups ready-to-eat baby-cut carrots, cut lengthwise into ¼-inch sticks

½ package (9-oz size) refrigerated linguine, cut into 2-inch pieces

⅓ cup chicken broth

1 tablespoon soy sauce

2 teaspoons cornstarch

1 teaspoon sugar

2 teaspoons finely chopped gingerroot

2 to 4 cloves garlic, finely chopped

2 teaspoons canola oil

½ cup thinly sliced red onion

Sesame seed, toasted, if desired*

1   Trim fat from pork. Cut pork with grain into 2 × 1-inch strips; cut strips across grain into ⅛-inch slices (pork is easier to cut if partially frozen, about 1½ hours). Remove strings from pea pods.

2   In 3-quart saucepan, heat 2 quarts water to boiling. Add pea pods, carrots and linguine; heat to boiling. Boil 2 to 3 minutes or just until linguine is tender; drain.

3   In small bowl, mix broth, soy sauce, cornstarch, sugar, gingerroot and garlic.

4   In 12-inch nonstick skillet or wok, heat oil over medium-high heat. Add pork and onion; stir-fry about 2 minutes or until pork is no longer pink. Stir broth mixture; stir into pork mixture. Stir in pea pods, carrots and linguine. Cook 2 minutes, stirring occasionally. Sprinkle with sesame seed.

*To toast sesame seed, sprinkle in ungreased heavy skillet. Cook over medium-low heat 5 to 7 minutes, stirring frequently until browning begins, then stirring constantly until golden brown.

Betty Tip

Being active helps lower blood glucose levels by making the body's cells more sensitive to insulin, so *fit in some workout time every day.*

1 Serving: Calories 270 (Calories from Fat 70); Total Fat 8g (Saturated Fat 2g; Trans Fat 0g); Cholesterol 35mg; Sodium 440mg; Total Carbohydrate 31g (Dietary Fiber 3g; Sugars 6g); Protein 19g **% Daily Value:** Vitamin A 160%; Vitamin C 20%; Calcium 4%; Iron 15% **Exchanges:** 1 Starch, ½ Other Carbohydrate, 1 Vegetable, 2 Lean Meat, ½ Fat

Maple Pork with Figs

5 ingredients

PREP TIME: **25 MINUTES** • START TO FINISH: **25 MINUTES** • 4 SERVINGS • *Carbohydrate Choices* **2**

4 bone-in pork loin chops,
  ½ inch thick (about
  1¼ lb), trimmed of fat

½ teaspoon salt

½ cup apple juice or dry red
  wine

¼ cup real maple syrup

⅓ cup coarsely chopped dried
  figs

1 teaspoon cornstarch

¼ cup water

1 Spray 12-inch skillet with cooking spray; heat skillet over medium-high heat. Sprinkle pork with salt; place in skillet. Cook about 5 minutes, turning once, until browned. Remove from skillet; keep warm.

2 In same skillet, cook apple juice, maple syrup and figs over medium-high heat 5 minutes, stirring frequently.

3 In small bowl, mix cornstarch and water; stir into juice mixture. Cook over medium-high heat about 2 minutes, stirring constantly, until thickened and clear.

4 Reduce heat to medium. Return pork to skillet; spoon sauce over pork. Simmer about 2 minutes or until pork is no longer pink in center.

Betty Tip

The apple, maple and figs add a tremendous flavor to the pork.

The pork is lovely with baked or mashed potatoes—try Roasted Sesame Asparagus (page 80) as your vegetable.

1 Serving: Calories 260 (Calories from Fat 70); Total Fat 8g (Saturated Fat 2.5g; Trans Fat 0g); Cholesterol 65mg; Sodium 340mg; Total Carbohydrate 26g (Dietary Fiber 1g; Sugars 21g); Protein 22g **% Daily Value:** Vitamin A 0%; Vitamin C 0%; Calcium 4%; Iron 8% **Exchanges:** 1½ Other Carbohydrate, 3 Lean Meat

Roasted Indian-Spiced Chicken

PREP TIME: **15 MINUTES** • START TO FINISH: **30 MINUTES** • 4 SERVINGS • *Carbohydrate Choices*

1 teaspoon ground cumin

1 teaspoon ground coriander

½ teaspoon salt

½ teaspoon fennel seed, crushed

½ teaspoon dried thyme leaves

½ teaspoon ground cinnamon

½ teaspoon pepper

1 tablespoon grated gingerroot

4 boneless skinless chicken breasts (about 1¼ lb)

½ cup mango chutney

1 Heat oven to 425°F. Line cookie sheet with foil. In shallow dish, mix cumin, coriander, salt, fennel, thyme, cinnamon and pepper.

2 Rub gingerroot on chicken, then coat chicken with spice mixture.

3 Spray 10-inch skillet with cooking spray; heat over medium heat. Add chicken; cook 2 to 3 minutes, turning once, until browned. Place chicken on cookie sheet.

4 Bake 10 to 12 minutes or until juice of chicken is clear when center of thickest part is cut (170°F).

5 Serve chicken with chutney (snip any large pieces of chutney with kitchen scissors).

Betty Tip

The herbs and spices lend a somewhat exotic flavor to this Indian-spiced chicken dish. The chutney adds a sweet/sour flavor.

As you may have guessed, rice is a great serve-with, as is Brown Rice–Veggie Salad (page 160).

1 Serving: Calories 210 (Calories from Fat 45); Total Fat 5g (Saturated Fat 1.5g; Trans Fat 0g); Cholesterol 85mg; Sodium 390mg; Total Carbohydrate 11g (Dietary Fiber 0g; Sugars 10g); Protein 32g **% Daily Value:** Vitamin A 2%; Vitamin C 4%; Calcium 4%; Iron 10% **Exchanges:** 1 Other Carbohydrate, 4 Very Lean Meat, ½ Fat

Lime- and Chili-Rubbed Chicken Breasts

PREP TIME: **20 MINUTES** • START TO FINISH: **20 MINUTES** • 4 SERVINGS • *Carbohydrate Choices* **0**

2 teaspoons chili powder

2 teaspoons packed brown sugar

2 teaspoons grated lime peel

½ teaspoon salt

¼ teaspoon garlic powder

⅛ teaspoon ground red pepper (cayenne)

4 boneless skinless chicken breasts (about 1¼ lb)

2 teaspoons olive or canola oil

1 Heat gas or charcoal grill. In small bowl, mix chili powder, brown sugar, lime peel, salt, garlic powder and ground red pepper. Rub both sides of chicken with oil, then with spice mixture.

2 Place chicken on grill over medium heat. Cover grill; cook 10 to 15 minutes, turning once or twice, until juice of chicken is clear when center of thickest part is cut (170°F).

Betty Tip

Refrigerating the "rubbed" chicken 20 to 30 minutes before grilling really enhances the flavor.

You can also bake the chicken. Place the rubbed chicken in a foil-lined shallow baking pan and bake in a 375°F oven for 25 to 30 minutes.

1 Serving: Calories 200 (Calories from Fat 60); Total Fat 7g (Saturated Fat 1.5g; Trans Fat 0g); Cholesterol 85mg; Sodium 390mg; Total Carbohydrate 3g (Dietary Fiber 0g; Sugars 2g); Protein 31g **% Daily Value:** Vitamin A 8%; Vitamin C 0%; Calcium 2%; Iron 8% **Exchanges:** 4½ Very Lean Meat, 1 Fat

Apricot-Almond Chicken

PREP TIME: **15 MINUTES** • START TO FINISH: **30 MINUTES** • 4 SERVINGS • *Carbohydrate Choices*

Cooking spray

4 boneless skinless chicken breasts (about 1¼ lb)

¼ teaspoon salt

⅛ teaspoon pepper

½ cup apricot preserves

1 tablespoon soy sauce

1 tablespoon Dijon mustard

½ cup sliced almonds

1 Heat oven to 425°F. Line 15 × 10 × 1-inch pan with foil; spray foil with cooking spray. Place chicken in pan; spray with cooking spray and sprinkle with salt and pepper. Bake 5 minutes.

2 Meanwhile, in small microwavable bowl, mix preserves, soy sauce and mustard; microwave on High 1 minute or until preserves are melted.

3 Stir presrves mixture and spoon over chicken; sprinkle evenly with almonds. Bake 10 to 15 minutes longer or until juice of chicken is clear when center of thickest part is cut (170°F).

Betty Tip

Save on prep and cleanup time by lining the pan with nonstick foil, available at most large supermarkets.

This baked chicken is wonderful served with Cranberry–Pine Nut Quinoa (page 148).

1 Serving: Calories 360 (Calories from Fat 100); Total Fat 11g (Saturated Fat 2g; Trans Fat 0g); Cholesterol 85mg; Sodium 560mg; Total Carbohydrate 30g (Dietary Fiber 2g; Sugars 20g); Protein 34g
% Daily Value: Vitamin A 0%; Vitamin C 4%; Calcium 6%; Iron 10% **Exchanges:** 2 Other Carbohydrate, 5 Very Lean Meat, 1½ Fat

Lemon Chicken with Olives

PREP TIME: **20 MINUTES** • START TO FINISH: **20 MINUTES** • 4 SERVINGS • *Carbohydrate Choices* 0

4 boneless skinless chicken breast halves (about 1¼ lb)

2 teaspoons olive or canola oil

1 tablespoon lemon juice

1 teaspoon salt-free lemon-pepper seasoning

¼ cup sliced ripe olives

4 thin slices lemon

1   Set oven control to broil. Spray broiler pan rack with cooking spray. Starting at thickest edge of each chicken breast, cut horizontally almost to opposite side. Open cut chicken breast so it is an even thickness.

2   In small bowl, mix oil and lemon juice. Drizzle over both sides of chicken breasts. Sprinkle both sides with lemon-pepper seasoning. Place on rack in broiler pan.

3   Broil with tops 4 inches from heat about 10 minutes, turning once, until chicken is no longer pink in center. During last 2 minutes of broiling, top with olives and lemon slices.

Betty Tip
To keep with the lemon theme, serve this chicken with Lemony Couscous with Spinach (page 154).

1 Serving: Calories 200 (Calories from Fat 70); Total Fat 8g (Saturated Fat 1.5g; Trans Fat 0g); Cholesterol 85mg; Sodium 150mg; Total Carbohydrate 1g (Dietary Fiber 0g; Sugars 0g); Protein 31g **% Daily Value:** Vitamin A 0%; Vitamin C 2%; Calcium 2%; Iron 8% **Exchanges:** 4½ Very Lean Meat, 1 Fat

Lemon-Pepper Halibut and Squash Packets

PREP TIME: **30 MINUTES** • START TO FINISH: **30 MINUTES** • 4 SERVINGS • *Carbohydrate Choices*

1 lb halibut fillets (½ to ¾ inch thick)

2 teaspoons dried basil leaves

1 teaspoon lemon-pepper seasoning

1 teaspoon seasoned salt

3 medium zucchini or yellow summer squash, cut into 2 × 1-inch strips

1 medium red bell pepper, cut into 1-inch pieces

2 tablespoons olive or canola oil

1 Heat gas or charcoal grill. Cut 4 (18 × 12-inch) sheets of heavy-duty foil; spray with cooking spray. Cut halibut into 4 serving pieces if necessary. Place 1 fish piece on center of each sheet. Sprinkle fillets with 1 teaspoon of the basil, ½ teaspoon of the lemon-pepper seasoning and ½ teaspoon of the seasoned salt. Arrange zucchini and bell pepper evenly over fish. Sprinkle with remaining basil, lemon-pepper seasoning and seasoned salt. Drizzle with oil.

2 Bring up 2 sides of foil over fish and vegetables so edges meet. Seal edges, making tight ½-inch fold; fold again, allowing space for heat circulation and expansion. Fold other sides to seal.

3 Place packets on grill over medium heat. Cover grill; cook 15 to 20 minutes, rotating packets ½ turn after 8 minutes, until fish flakes easily with fork and vegetables are tender. To serve, cut large X across top of each packet; carefully fold back foil to allow steam to escape.

Betty Tip

If you like salmon, use salmon fillets instead of the halibut. You can also use 1 to 2 tablespoons of chopped fresh basil leaves instead of the dried basil.

1 Serving: Calories 200 (Calories from Fat 80); Total Fat 9g (Saturated Fat 1.5g; Trans Fat 0g); Cholesterol 60mg; Sodium 540mg; Total Carbohydrate 7g (Dietary Fiber 2g; Sugars 4g); Protein 24g **% Daily Value:** Vitamin A 25%; Vitamin C 70%; Calcium 4%; Iron 6% **Exchanges:** 1 Vegetable, 3 Lean Meat

Baked Fish Packets with Chinese Parsley Paste

PREP TIME: **30 MINUTES** • START TO FINISH: **30 MINUTES** • 4 SERVINGS • *Carbohydrate Choices* ½

FISH

1 lb cod, flounder or red snapper fillets

½ lb daikon radish, peeled, thinly sliced

1 lb fresh asparagus spears, cut into 1-inch pieces

¼ cup dry sherry or chicken broth

½ teaspoon salt

PARSLEY PASTE

1 cup fresh cilantro leaves

1 cup fresh parsley sprigs

2 tablespoons lemon juice

1 tablespoon canola oil

½ teaspoon grated gingerroot

¼ teaspoon grated lemon peel

1 green onion, cut into 1-inch pieces

3 cloves garlic, cut in half

Dash salt, if desired

GARNISH, IF DESIRED

Pine nuts, toasted

1   Heat oven to 425°F. Cut fish into 4 serving pieces. Cut 4 (18 × 12-inch) sheets of heavy-duty foil. Divide radish and asparagus evenly among and on center of each sheet. Sprinkle each with 1 tablespoon of the sherry and ⅛ teaspoon of the salt. Top with fish. Bring up 2 sides of foil so edges meet. Seal edges, making tight ½-inch fold; fold again, allowing space for heat circulation and expansion. Fold other sides to seal.

2   Place packets on ungreased cookie sheet. Bake about 15 minutes or until fish flakes easily with fork.

3   Meanwhile, place all parsley paste ingredients in blender. Cover; blend on medium to high speed, stopping blender frequently to scrape sides, until smooth.

4   To serve, cut large X across top of each packet; carefully fold back foil to allow steam to escape. Spoon about 2 tablespoons parsley paste over each serving. Garnish with pine nuts.

Betty Tip

To toast pine nuts, sprinkle in ungreased heavy skillet. Cook over medium heat 5 to 7 minutes, stirring frequently until nuts begin to brown, then stirring constantly until nuts are light brown.

Serve this flavorful fish on a bed of whole wheat pasta or brown rice.

1 Serving: Calories 170 (Calories from Fat 45); Total Fat 5g (Saturated Fat 0.5g; Trans Fat 0g); Cholesterol 60mg; Sodium 410mg; Total Carbohydrate 7g (Dietary Fiber 3g; Sugars 3g); Protein 24g **% Daily Value:** Vitamin A 40%; Vitamin C 30%; Calcium 8%; Iron 15% **Exchanges:** 1½ Vegetable, 3 Very Lean Meat, ½ Fat

Pecan-Crusted Catfish

PREP TIME: **10 MINUTES** • START TO FINISH: **30 MINUTES** • 4 SERVINGS • *Carbohydrate Choices* ½

½ cup corn flake crumbs

¼ cup finely ground pecans (1 oz)

¼ teaspoon paprika

⅛ teaspoon garlic powder

⅛ teaspoon ground red pepper (cayenne)

1 egg white

1 lb catfish, haddock, orange roughy, sole, flounder or other medium-firm fish fillets (about ¾ inch thick), cut into 4 serving pieces

1 Heat oven to 450°F. Spray 15 × 10 × 1-inch pan with cooking spray. In large resealable food-storage plastic bag, mix corn flake crumbs, pecans, paprika, garlic powder and ground red pepper.

2 In shallow dish or pie plate, beat egg white slightly with fork. Dip fish into egg white, then place in bag. Seal bag and shake until evenly coated. Place in pan.

3 Bake 15 to 20 minutes or until fish flakes easily with fork.

Betty Tip

The American Heart Association recommends eating two fish meals a week—a recipe like this makes that goal easy.

1 Serving: Calories 240 (Calories from Fat 110); Total Fat 12g (Saturated Fat 2g; Trans Fat 0g); Cholesterol 85mg; Sodium 115mg; Total Carbohydrate 6g (Dietary Fiber 0g; Sugars 0g); Protein 25g **% Daily Value:** Vitamin A 4%; Vitamin C 2%; Calcium 6%; Iron 20% **Exchanges:** ½ Starch, 3½ Lean Meat

Walnut-Crusted Salmon

PREP TIME: **15 MINUTES** • START TO FINISH: **30 MINUTES** • 4 SERVINGS • *Carbohydrate Choices* 1

2 slices firm whole wheat
  bread

3 tablespoons finely chopped
  walnuts (about 1 oz)

2 teaspoons olive or
  canola oil

½ teaspoon dried thyme
  leaves

4 teaspoons Dijon mustard

4 teaspoons honey

1¼ lb salmon fillets, cut into
  4 serving pieces

1 Heat oven to 400°F. Spray cookie sheet with cooking spray. Grate bread on large side of a box grater. In small bowl, mix bread crumbs, walnuts, oil and thyme.

2 In another small bowl, mix mustard and honey; spread over tops of salmon pieces. Sprinkle with bread crumb mixture, pressing gently so crumbs adhere. Place on cookie sheet.

3 Bake 12 to 14 minutes or until salmon flakes easily with fork and topping is lightly browned.

Betty Tip
A food processor easily makes bread crumbs and chops the walnuts. Tear the bread into pieces and place it in the processor work bowl with the walnuts.

1 Serving: Calories 320 (Calories from Fat 130); Total Fat 15g (Saturated Fat 3g; Trans Fat 0g); Cholesterol 95mg; Sodium 280mg; Total Carbohydrate 13g (Dietary Fiber 1g; Sugars 7g); Protein 33g **% Daily Value:** Vitamin A 4%; Vitamin C 2%; Calcium 4%; Iron 10% **Exchanges:** ½ Starch, ½ Other Carbohydrate, 4½ Lean Meat

Basil Salmon and Julienne Vegetables

PREP TIME: **15 MINUTES** • START TO FINISH: **25 MINUTES** • 4 SERVINGS • *Carbohydrate Choices* 1

1 tablespoon butter or margarine

1 bag (1 lb) frozen bell pepper and onion stir-fry

1 medium zucchini, cut into julienne (matchstick-size) strips

4 salmon fillets (4 to 5 oz each)

2 tablespoons chopped fresh basil leaves

½ teaspoon seasoned salt

1 teaspoon lemon-pepper seasoning

¼ cup chicken broth

1   In 12-inch nonstick skillet, melt butter over medium heat. Add bell pepper stir-fry. Cook and stir 2 minutes. Stir in zucchini.

2   Place salmon, skin side down, in skillet, pushing down into vegetables if necessary. Sprinkle salmon and vegetables with basil, seasoned salt and lemon-pepper seasoning. Pour broth over salmon and vegetables.

3   Reduce heat to medium-low; cover and cook 8 to 10 minutes or until salmon flakes easily with fork. Remove salmon and vegetables from skillet with slotted spoon.

Betty Tip

If you purchase one large salmon fillet, just cut it into serving-size pieces before cooking—you can also make the recipe with salmon steaks.

1 Serving: Calories 240 (Calories from Fat 90); Total Fat 10g (Saturated Fat 3.5g; Trans Fat 0g); Cholesterol 80mg; Sodium 420mg; Total Carbohydrate 12g (Dietary Fiber 2g; Sugars 6g); Protein 26g **% Daily Value:** Vitamin A 10%; Vitamin C 40%; Calcium 4%; Iron 8% **Exchanges:** ½ Other Carbohydrate, 1 Vegetable, 3½ Lean Meat

Green Pepper– and Tomato-Topped Snapper

PREP TIME: 30 MINUTES • **START TO FINISH: 30 MINUTES** • 4 SERVINGS • *Carbohydrate Choices* 2

1 medium onion, coarsely chopped (⅔ cup)

½ medium green bell pepper, coarsely chopped (½ cup)

2 medium tomatoes, coarsely chopped (1½ cups)

4 medium green onions, thinly sliced (¼ cup)

2 tablespoons red wine vinegar

½ teaspoon salt

½ teaspoon dried thyme leaves

¼ teaspoon red pepper sauce

1 cup uncooked instant brown rice

2 cups water

1½ lb red snapper, sole or flounder fillets (about ½ inch thick)

Cooking spray

2 tablespoons chopped fresh parsley

1   Heat gas or charcoal grill. Cut 1 (24 × 18-inch) sheet of heavy-duty foil; spray with cooking spray. Layer coarsely chopped onion, bell pepper and tomatoes on center of sheet. Bring up 2 sides of foil over vegetables so edges meet. Seal edges, making tight ½-inch fold; fold again, allowing space for heat circulation and expansion. Fold other sides to seal.

2   Place vegetable packet on grill over medium heat. Cover grill; cook 6 minutes, turning once. Meanwhile, in large bowl, mix green onions, vinegar, salt, thyme and pepper sauce; set aside. Cook rice in water as directed on package.

3   Spray fish and grill basket that has locking top with cooking spray. Place fish in basket. Place on grill with vegetable packet. Rotate vegetable packet ½ turn. Cover grill; cook 8 to 12 minutes, turning fish once, until fish flakes easily with fork.

4   Place fish on serving platter; keep warm. Cut large X across top of packet; carefully fold back foil to allow steam to escape. Add grilled vegetables and parsley to green onion mixture; toss. Spoon over fish. Serve with rice.

Betty Tip

It's easy to vary this recipe, depending on what you have on hand. You can use any color of bell pepper, any variety of tomato and any choice of fish listed in the recipe.

1 Serving: Calories 290 (Calories from Fat 35); Total Fat 4g (Saturated Fat 0.5g; Trans Fat 0g); Cholesterol 90mg; Sodium 460mg; Total Carbohydrate 28g (Dietary Fiber 3g; Sugars 4g); Protein 35g **% Daily Value:** Vitamin A 20%; Vitamin C 20%; Calcium 6%; Iron 8% **Exchanges:** 2 Starch, 4 Very Lean Meat

Tuna with Three-Herb Pesto

PREP TIME: **25 MINUTES** • START TO FINISH: **25 MINUTES** • 4 SERVINGS (WITH 3 TABLESPOONS PESTO EACH) •

Carbohydrate Choices 0

1 lb tuna steaks

1 teaspoon olive or canola oil

¼ teaspoon salt

1 cup loosely packed fresh
  cilantro leaves

½ cup loosely packed fresh
  flat-leaf parsley leaves

¼ cup loosely packed fresh
  basil leaves

4 medium green onions,
  sliced (¼ cup)

1 clove garlic, cut in half

2 tablespoons lime juice

2 teaspoons olive or
  canola oil

¼ teaspoon salt

¼ cup reduced-sodium
  chicken broth

1 tablespoon grated
  Parmesan cheese

1 Set oven control to broil. Brush both sides of tuna steaks with
1 teaspoon oil. Place on rack in broiler pan. Broil with tops 4 inches
from heat 8 to 10 minutes, turning once and sprinkling with ¼ teaspoon
salt, until tuna flakes easily with fork and is slightly pink in center.

2 Meanwhile, in food processor bowl with metal blade, place
remaining ingredients except broth and cheese. Cover; process about
10 seconds or until finely chopped. With processor running, slowly pour
in broth and continue processing until almost smooth. Stir in cheese.
Serve with tuna.

Betty Tip

Cook tuna just until it flakes since it's easy to overcook. It
sometimes retains a slightly pink color, even when it's flaky
and thoroughly cooked.

1 Serving: Calories 190 (Calories from Fat 90); Total Fat 10g (Saturated Fat 2.5g; Trans Fat 0g);
Cholesterol 70mg; Sodium 430mg; Total Carbohydrate 3g (Dietary Fiber 0g; Sugars 0g); Protein 23g
% Daily Value: Vitamin A 25%; Vitamin C 15%; Calcium 6%; Iron 10% **Exchanges:** 3½ Very Lean Meat,
1½ Fat

Italian-Style Tilapia Fillets

20 minutes

PREP TIME: **15 MINUTES** • START TO FINISH: **15 MINUTES** • 4 SERVINGS (1 FILLET AND ½ CUP TOMATO MIXTURE EACH) •

Carbohydrate Choices 0

1 lb tilapia or catfish fillets, cut into 4 serving pieces

1 teaspoon salt-free seasoning blend

1 tablespoon olive or canola oil

1 clove garlic, finely chopped

1 pint (2 cups) cherry tomatoes, cut in half

¼ cup sliced ripe olives, drained

1 Sprinkle both sides of fish fillets with seasoning blend. In 12-inch nonstick skillet, heat oil over medium-high heat. Add fish; cook 6 to 8 minutes, turning once, until golden. Remove fish from skillet; cover to keep warm.

2 Heat same skillet over medium-high heat. Add garlic; cook and stir 30 seconds. Add tomatoes; cook about 3 minutes, stirring occasionally, until softened and juicy. Stir in olives. Serve over fish.

Betty Tip

Tilapia and catfish are farm-raised and reliably available year-round, but any mild-tasting fish fillets—say, Alaskan pollock or cod—will also work nicely.

1 Serving: Calories 160 (Calories from Fat 50); Total Fat 6g (Saturated Fat 1g; Trans Fat 0g); Cholesterol 60mg; Sodium 170mg; Total Carbohydrate 4g (Dietary Fiber 1g; Sugars 2g); Protein 22g
% Daily Value: Vitamin A 15%; Vitamin C 10%; Calcium 4%; Iron 4% **Exchanges:** 3 Very Lean Meat, 1 Fat

Chicken–Wild Rice Salad with
Dried Cherries   *Page 146*

Grains and Beans

6

Apple-Rosemary Pork and Barley

PREP TIME: **25 MINUTES** • START TO FINISH: **25 MINUTES** • 4 SERVINGS • *Carbohydrate Choices* **3**

1½ cups water

¾ cup uncooked quick-cooking barley

2 tablespoons chopped fresh or 2 teaspoons dried rosemary leaves, crushed

1 pork tenderloin (¾ lb)

2 teaspoons canola or soybean oil

1 medium onion, chopped (½ cup)

1 clove garlic, finely chopped

¼ cup apple jelly

1 medium unpeeled red cooking apple, sliced

1 In 2-quart saucepan, heat water to boiling. Stir in barley and 1 tablespoon of the rosemary. Reduce heat to low; cover and simmer 10 to 12 minutes or until liquid is absorbed and barley is tender.

2 Meanwhile, cut pork in half lengthwise, then into ¼-inch-thick slices.

3 In 10-inch nonstick skillet, heat oil over medium-high heat. Add pork, onion, garlic and remaining 1 tablespoon rosemary; cook about 8 to 10 minutes, stirring frequently, until pork is no longer pink in center. Stir in apple jelly and apple slices; cook until hot. Serve over barley.

Betty Tip

You can get quite an assortment of phytochemicals—naturally occurring plant chemicals—by eating the whole food including the peel; that's why we left the peel on the apple slices.

1 Serving: Calories 350 (Calories from Fat 60); Total Fat 6g (Saturated Fat 1.5g; Trans Fat 0g); Cholesterol 55mg; Sodium 50mg; Total Carbohydrate 50g (Dietary Fiber 7g; Sugars 14g); Protein 23g **% Daily Value:** Vitamin A 0%; Vitamin C 4%; Calcium 4%; Iron 10% **Exchanges:** 2½ Starch, 1 Other Carbohydrate, 2 Very Lean Meat, ½ Fat

Penne with Spinach and Ham

PREP TIME: **25 MINUTES** • START TO FINISH: **25 MINUTES** • 4 SERVINGS • *Carbohydrate Choices* **3**

2⅔ cups uncooked whole wheat penne pasta (8 oz)

2 teaspoons olive oil

1 medium onion, chopped (½ cup)

4 cloves garlic, finely chopped

1½ cups grape tomatoes or halved cherry tomatoes

⅔ cup finely chopped cooked ham

½ cup dry white wine or water

4 cups fresh spinach leaves

2 tablespoons finely shredded Parmesan cheese

1 Cook and drain pasta as directed on package, omitting salt.

2 Meanwhile, in 10-inch nonstick skillet, heat oil over medium heat. Add onion and garlic; cook 3 to 4 minutes, stirring occasionally, until onion is tender. Stir in tomatoes, ham and wine. Cook and stir until some of the wine has evaporated.

3 Add spinach and pasta; toss gently. Sprinkle with cheese.

Betty Tip

By dicing the ham into small pieces, the flavor penetrates every bite without adding too much sodium.

At 3 carb choices, this is almost a meal in itself—just add a glass of skim milk.

1 Serving: Calories 310 (Calories from Fat 60); Total Fat 6g (Saturated Fat 2g; Trans Fat 0g); Cholesterol 15mg; Sodium 610mg; Total Carbohydrate 46g (Dietary Fiber 6g; Sugars 4g); Protein 16g **% Daily Value:** Vitamin A 70%; Vitamin C 15%; Calcium 10%; Iron 15% **Exchanges:** 2½ Starch, 1 Vegetable, 1 Very Lean Meat, 1 Fat

Chicken and Veggies with Bulgur

PREP TIME: **25 MINUTES** • START TO FINISH: **30 MINUTES** • 4 SERVINGS (1 CUP EACH) • *Carbohydrate Choices* 2

2 cups chicken broth

1 cup uncooked bulgur wheat

½ teaspoon dried dill weed

¼ teaspoon garlic salt

½ lb boneless skinless chicken breasts, cut into ¾-inch pieces

2 teaspoons canola oil

2½ cups thinly sliced zucchini or carrots (about 2 medium zucchini or 5 medium carrots)

1 medium onion, cut in half lengthwise, then cut crosswise into thin slices

1 In 1½-quart saucepan, heat broth to boiling. Stir in bulgur, dill weed and garlic salt. Reduce heat to low; cover and simmer 20 to 25 minutes or until bulgur is tender. Remove from heat.

2 Meanwhile, spray 10-inch skillet with cooking spray; heat over medium-high heat. Add chicken; cook about 4 minutes, stirring frequently, until no longer pink in center. Remove chicken from skillet; keep warm.

3 Add oil to skillet; rotate skillet to coat with oil. Add zucchini and onion; cook about 4 to 5 minutes, stirring frequently, until vegetables are crisp-tender. Stir in chicken. Toss with cooked bulgur.

Betty Tip
Bulgur wheat is a great grain to serve for a weeknight dinner because it cooks in only 20 minutes.

1 Serving: Calories 260 (Calories from Fat 50); Total Fat 5g (Saturated Fat 1g; Trans Fat 0g); Cholesterol 35mg; Sodium 620mg; Total Carbohydrate 32g (Dietary Fiber 7g; Sugars 3g); Protein 20g **% Daily Value:** Vitamin A 4%; Vitamin C 10%; Calcium 4%; Iron 10% **Exchanges:** 1½ Starch, ½ Other Carbohydrate, 1 Vegetable, 2 Very Lean Meat, ½ Fat

Asian Chicken and Millet Stir-Fry

PREP TIME: **30 MINUTES** • START TO FINISH: **30 MINUTES** • 6 SERVINGS ($1^2/_3$ CUPS EACH) • *Carbohydrate Choices* **3**

2¼ cups fat-free chicken broth with 33% less sodium

1 cup uncooked millet

2 bags (1 lb each) frozen broccoli, red peppers, onions and mushrooms (or other combination), thawed, drained

1⅓ cups apple juice

¼ cup reduced-sodium soy sauce

2 tablespoons cornstarch

½ teaspoon ground ginger

2 cups cut-up cooked chicken or turkey

1 In 2-quart saucepan, heat broth to boiling. Reduce heat; stir in millet. Cover; simmer 20 minutes.

2 Meanwhile, spray 12-inch skillet with cooking spray; heat over medium-high heat. Add vegetables and ⅓ cup of the apple juice. Reduce heat to medium; cover and; cook 2 to 3 minutes or until vegetables are crisp-tender.

3 In small bowl, mix remaining 1 cup apple juice, the soy sauce, cornstarch and ginger. Gradually stir juice mixture into vegetable mixture. Heat to boiling, stirring constantly. Boil and stir 1 minute.

4 Stir chicken into vegetable mixture; cook about 2 minutes or until thoroughly heated. Toss with cooked millet.

Betty Tip

This excellent main-dish stir-fry uses millet, a whole grain that's been around for centuries and cooks quickly—what's not to love?

1 Serving: Calories 320 (Calories from Fat 45); Total Fat 5g (Saturated Fat 1g; Trans Fat 0g); Cholesterol 40mg; Sodium 620mg; Total Carbohydrate 45g (Dietary Fiber 7g; Sugars 9g); Protein 22g **% Daily Value:** Vitamin A 30%; Vitamin C 40%; Calcium 6%; Iron 20% **Exchanges:** 1 Starch, 1 Other Carbohydrate, 3 Vegetable, 2 Lean Meat

Chicken–Wild Rice Salad with Dried Cherries

PREP TIME: **30 MINUTES** • START TO FINISH: **30 MINUTES** • 5 SERVINGS (1¼ CUPS EACH) • *Carbohydrate Choices* **3**

1 package (6.2 oz) fast-cooking long-grain and wild rice mix

2 cups chopped cooked chicken or turkey

1 medium unpeeled eating apple, chopped (1 cup)

1 medium green bell pepper, chopped (1 cup)

1 medium stalk celery, chopped (½ cup)

½ cup chopped dried apricots

⅓ cup chopped dried cherries

2 tablespoons soy sauce

2 tablespoons water

2 teaspoons sugar

2 teaspoons cider vinegar

⅓ cup dry-roasted peanuts

1   Cook rice mix as directed on package, omitting butter. On large cookie sheet, spread rice evenly in thin layer. Let stand 10 minutes, stirring occasionally, until cool.

2   Meanwhile, in large bowl, mix chicken, apple, bell pepper, celery, apricots and cherries. In small bowl, mix soy sauce, water, sugar and vinegar until sugar is dissolved.

3   Add rice and soy sauce mixture to apple mixture; toss gently until coated. Add peanuts; toss gently.

Betty Tip

A terrific main dish with a yummy combination of ingredients—turn up the heat by sprinkling in ¼ teaspoon of crushed red pepper flakes.

1 Serving: Calories 380 (Calories from Fat 90); Total Fat 10g (Saturated Fat 2g; Trans Fat 0g); Cholesterol 50mg; Sodium 950mg; Total Carbohydrate 50g (Dietary Fiber 4g; Sugars 18g); Protein 23g **% Daily Value:** Vitamin A 20%; Vitamin C 45%; Calcium 6%; Iron 15% **Exchanges:** 1½ Starch, 1½ Other Carbohydrate, 1 Vegetable, 2½ Lean Meat

Spinach-Shrimp Pizza

PREP TIME: 15 MINUTES • START TO FINISH: **30 MINUTES** • 4 SERVINGS • *Carbohydrate Choices* **2½**

4 whole-grain pita breads (6 inch)

1 container (4 oz) reduced-fat garlic-and-herbs spreadable cheese

1 tablespoon fat-free (skim) milk

1 cup lightly packed spinach leaves, coarsely chopped

2 tablespoons chopped fresh or 1 teaspoon dried basil leaves

1 cup sliced fresh mushrooms

²/₃ cup chopped tomato

½ cup frozen cooked salad shrimp (from 4-oz bag), thawed, well drained

½ cup shredded mozzarella cheese (2 oz)

2 tablespoons finely shredded Parmesan cheese

1 Heat oven to 400°F. On large cookie sheet, arrange pita breads.

2 In small bowl, mix cheese and milk. Stir in spinach and basil. Spread over each pita bread to within ½ inch of edge. Top with mushrooms, tomato, shrimp and cheeses.

3 Bake 10 to 15 minutes or until cheese is melted.

Betty Tip

Cut these pizzas into small wedges to serve as an appetizer. When serving as a main dish, try Melon and Grape Salad (page 76) or any fresh fruit for a refreshing accompaniment.

1 Serving: Calories 310 (Calories from Fat 90); Total Fat 10g (Saturated Fat 6g; Trans Fat 0g); Cholesterol 60mg; Sodium 700mg; Total Carbohydrate 37g (Dietary Fiber 5g; Sugars 10g); Protein 18g **% Daily Value:** Vitamin A 25%; Vitamin C 6%; Calcium 30%; Iron 15% **Exchanges:** 1½ Starch, 1 Other Carbohydrate, 2 Lean Meat, ½ Fat

Cranberry–Pine Nut Quinoa

PREP TIME: **20 MINUTES** • START TO FINISH: **30 MINUTES** • 8 SERVINGS (½ CUP EACH) • *Carbohydrate Choices* **2**

1 cup uncooked red or white quinoa

1 tablespoon butter or margarine

¼ cup chopped red onion

⅓ cup chopped celery

½ cup coarsely chopped baking apple

1½ cups roasted vegetable stock (from 32-oz container) or chicken broth

½ cup orange juice

1 jar (1¾ oz) pine nuts (about ⅓ cup)

½ cup sweetened dried cranberries

¼ cup shredded Parmesan cheese (1 oz)

¼ teaspoon salt

2 tablespoons finely chopped parsley

1 Rinse quinoa thoroughly by placing in a fine-mesh strainer and holding under cold running water until water runs clear, about 2 minutes; drain well.

2 In 2-quart saucepan, melt butter over medium heat. Add onion, celery, apple and quinoa; cook 5 minutes, stirring occasionally.

3 Stir in vegetable stock and orange juice. Heat to boiling. Reduce heat; cover and simmer 15 to 20 minutes or until all liquid is absorbed and quinoa is tender.

4 Meanwhile, heat oven to 350°F. Spread pine nuts in ungreased shallow pan. Bake 3 to 6 minutes, stirring occasionally, until light golden brown.

5 Fluff quinoa with fork. Stir in cranberries, pine nuts, cheese and salt. Sprinkle with parsley.

Betty Tip

Once you get used to eating grains, you'll want to serve them often. This flavorful grain dish can be served warm or cold.

If you'd like to reduce the saturated fat, use canola oil instead of butter.

1 Serving: Calories 190 (Calories from Fat 60); Total Fat 7g (Saturated Fat 2g; Trans Fat 0g); Cholesterol 5mg; Sodium 340mg; Total Carbohydrate 26g (Dietary Fiber 2g; Sugars 10g); Protein 5g **% Daily Value:** Vitamin A 8%; Vitamin C 8%; Calcium 6%; Iron 15% **Exchanges:** ½ Starch, 1 Other Carbohydrate, ½ High-Fat Meat, ½ Fat

Quinoa with Black Beans

PREP TIME: **30 MINUTES** • START TO FINISH: **30 MINUTES** • 8 SERVINGS (½ CUP EACH) • *Carbohydrate Choices* 1½

1 cup uncooked quinoa

2 cups chicken or vegetable broth

1 cup black beans (from 15-oz can), drained, rinsed

½ cup frozen whole kernel corn, thawed

1 small tomato, chopped (½ cup)

¼ cup chopped fresh cilantro

4 medium green onions, chopped (¼ cup)

1 tablespoon fresh lime juice

1 clove garlic, finely chopped

¼ teaspoon salt

1 Rinse quinoa thoroughly by placing in a fine-mesh strainer and holding under cold running water until water runs clear; drain well.

2 In 2-quart saucepan, heat broth to boiling. Add quinoa; reduce heat to low. Cover; simmer 15 to 20 minutes or until liquid is absorbed.

3 Fluff quinoa with fork. Stir in remaining ingredients. Cook uncovered about 3 minutes, stirring occasionally, until thoroughly heated.

Betty Tip

Quinoa is high in protein, low in fat and cooks quickly, making it a great grain to use.

As is, this recipe works well as a side dish; to make it a main dish, double the serving size.

1 Serving: Calories 130 (Calories from Fat 15); Total Fat 2g (Saturated Fat 0g; Trans Fat 0g); Cholesterol 0mg; Sodium 340mg; Total Carbohydrate 23g (Dietary Fiber 4g; Sugars 2g); Protein 6g **% Daily Value:** Vitamin A 4%; Vitamin C 2%; Calcium 4%; Iron 15% **Exchanges:** 1½ Starch

Edamame-Tabbouleh Salad

20 minutes

PREP TIME: **20 MINUTES** • START TO FINISH: **20 MINUTES** • 6 SERVINGS (1 CUP EACH) • *Carbohydrate Choices* 2

SALAD

1 package (5.8 oz) roasted garlic and olive oil couscous mix

1¼ cups water

1 teaspoon olive or canola oil

1 bag (10 oz) refrigerated fully cooked ready-to-eat shelled edamame (soybeans)

2 medium tomatoes, seeded, chopped (1½ cups)

1 small cucumber, peeled, chopped (1 cup)

¼ cup chopped fresh parsley

DRESSING

1 teaspoon grated lemon peel

2 tablespoons fresh lemon juice

1 teaspoon olive or canola oil

1 Make couscous mix as directed on package, using water and 1 teaspoon oil.

2 In large bowl, mix couscous and remaining salad ingredients. In small bowl, mix dressing ingredients. Pour dressing over salad; mix well. Serve immediately, or cover and refrigerate until serving time.

Betty Tip

You can use leftover tabbouleh salad to create a quick and easy lunch. Just spread the inside of a pita bread pocket with hummus and fill with the salad.

1 Serving: Calories 200 (Calories from Fat 46); Total Fat 6g (Saturated Fat 0g; Trans Fat 0g); Cholesterol 0mg; Sodium 294mg; Total Carbohydrate 28g (Dietary Fiber 4g; Sugars 4g); Protein 10g **% Daily Value:** Vitamin A 15%; Vitamin C 35%; Calcium 6%; Iron 10% **Exchanges:** 2 Starch, 1 Fat

Bulgur Pilaf with Pea Pods

PREP TIME: **30 MINUTES** • START TO FINISH: **30 MINUTES** • 4 SERVINGS (1 CUP EACH) • *Carbohydrate Choices* **2**

1 can (14 oz) chicken broth

½ cup water

1 teaspoon dried thyme
   leaves

1 cup uncooked bulgur wheat

1 teaspoon canola or
   soybean oil

1 cup fresh sugar snap peas,
   cut into ¾-inch pieces

½ cup finely chopped red bell
   pepper

⅓ cup sliced green onions
   (about 5 medium)

1 In 2-quart saucepan, heat broth, water and thyme to boiling. Stir in bulgur. Cover; simmer 15 to 20 minutes, stirring occasionally, until bulgur is tender and water is absorbed.

2 Meanwhile, in 8-inch skillet, heat oil over medium-high heat. Add sugar snap peas, bell pepper and onions; cook 3 to 4 minutes, stirring frequently, until tender.

3 Stir snap pea mixture into cooked bulgur.

Betty Tip

Serve this bulgur pilaf with your favorite fish or seafood recipe—add a citrus fruit salad and whole-grain bread and dinner is served.

1 Serving: Calories 165 (Calories from Fat 22); Total Fat 2g (Saturated Fat 0g; Trans Fat 0g); Cholesterol 0mg; Sodium 450mg; Total Carbohydrate 30g (Dietary Fiber 8g; Sugars 2g); Protein 8g
% Daily Value: Vitamin A 15%; Vitamin C 35%; Calcium 2%; Iron 8% **Exchanges:** 2 Starch

Lemony Couscous with Spinach

PREP TIME: **25 MINUTES** • START TO FINISH: **30 MINUTES** • 4 SERVINGS ($^2/_3$ CUP EACH) • *Carbohydrate Choices* **2½**

1 small green bell pepper, finely chopped (½ cup)

1 small onion, finely chopped (¼ cup)

⅓ cup finely chopped celery

2 teaspoons olive oil

2 teaspoons lemon juice

1 cup chicken or vegetable broth

1 cup uncooked whole wheat couscous

3 cups lightly packed fresh baby spinach leaves

2 teaspoons grated lemon peel

⅛ teaspoon pepper

1   In 3-quart saucepan, cook bell pepper, onion, celery, oil and lemon juice over medium heat about 4 minutes, stirring occasionally, until vegetables are crisp-tender.

2   Stir in broth. Heat to boiling. Stir in couscous, spinach, lemon peel and pepper. Remove from heat. Cover; let stand 5 minutes. Uncover; fluff with fork.

Betty Tip

Couscous makes a terrific side dish because it's so quick to prepare; this version with fresh lemon and veggies is not only tasty but pretty, too.

1 Serving: Calories 225 (Calories from Fat 30); Total Fat 4g (Saturated Fat 0g; Trans Fat 0g); Cholesterol 0mg; Sodium 285mg; Total Carbohydrate 39g (Dietary Fiber 4.5g; Sugars 1.5g); Protein 9g **% Daily Value:** Vitamin A 45%; Vitamin C 20%; Calcium 6%; Iron 12% **Exchanges:** 2 Starch, 1 Vegetable, 1 Fat

Couscous, Corn and Lima Bean Sauté

PREP TIME: **20 MINUTES** • START TO FINISH: **25 MINUTES** • 8 SERVINGS (1¼ CUPS EACH) • *Carbohydrate Choices* 4

1 tablespoon butter or
    margarine

1 large onion, chopped
    (1 cup)

1 clove garlic, finely chopped

1 box (12 oz) whole wheat
    couscous

1 box (10 oz) frozen whole
    kernel corn, thawed

2 boxes (9 oz each) frozen
    baby lima beans, thawed

2 cups water

1 tablespoon chopped fresh
    or 1 teaspoon dried thyme
    leaves

1 teaspoon salt

⅓ cup slivered almonds,
    toasted*

1   In 12-inch skillet, melt butter over medium-high heat. Add onion and garlic; cook about 2 minutes, stirring occasionally, until onion is crisp-tender.

2   Stir in remaining ingredients except almonds. Heat to boiling over high heat. Remove from heat; let stand 5 minutes. Fluff before serving. Sprinkle with almonds.

*To toast almonds, sprinkle in ungreased heavy skillet. Cook over medium heat 5 to 7 minutes, stirring frequently until almonds begin to brown, then stirring constantly until light brown.

Betty Tip

This recipe goes together in just minutes, thanks to whole wheat couscous, a whole grain that has already been cooked and dried. All you need to do is add veggies and water, heat to boiling, let stand and fluff. Now that's a real time savings!

1 Serving: Calories 320 (Calories from Fat 40); Total Fat 4.5g (Saturated Fat 1g; Trans Fat 0g); Cholesterol 0mg; Sodium 350mg; Total Carbohydrate 58g (Dietary Fiber 9g; Sugars 3g); Protein 12g **% Daily Value:** Vitamin A 6%; Vitamin C 10%; Calcium 6%; Iron 15% **Exchanges:** 4 Starch

Curried Coconut Couscous

PREP TIME: **15 MINUTES** • START TO FINISH: **20 MINUTES** • 6 SERVINGS ($^2/_3$ CUP EACH) • *Carbohydrate Choices* 2½

2 teaspoons olive oil

1 medium onion, thinly sliced (½ cup)

2 cloves garlic, finely chopped

1 teaspoon grated gingerroot

¾ cup chicken or vegetable broth

½ cup canned reduced-fat coconut milk (not cream of coconut)

1 teaspoon curry powder

¼ teaspoon salt

Dash ground red pepper (cayenne)

1 cup uncooked whole wheat couscous

⅓ cup golden raisins

1 In 2-quart saucepan, heat oil over medium heat. Add onion, garlic and gingerroot; cook 1 minute, stirring constantly.

2 Stir in broth, coconut milk, curry powder, salt and red pepper. Heat to boiling. Stir in couscous and raisins. Remove from heat. Cover; let stand 5 minutes. Uncover; fluff with fork.

Betty Tip

Curry and coconut team up to make a terrific-tasting grain side dish; serve with Roasted Indian-Spiced Chicken (page 127) or Pork with Caramelized Onions (page 121).

1 Serving: Calories 185 (Calories from Fat 26); Total Fat 3g (Saturated Fat 1g; Trans Fat 0g); Cholesterol 0mg; Sodium 240mg; Total Carbohydrate 38g (Dietary Fiber 4g; Sugars 5g); Protein 5g **% Daily Value:** Vitamin A 0%; Vitamin C 0%; Calcium 0%; Iron 8% **Exchanges:** 2 Starch, 1 Fat

Spicy Couscous and Chickpea Salad

20 minutes

PREP TIME: **20 MINUTES** • START TO FINISH: **20 MINUTES** • 4 SERVINGS (1-CUP EACH) • *Carbohydrate Choices* 3

SALAD

½ cup uncooked whole wheat couscous

1½ cups water

¼ teaspoon salt

1 can (15 oz) chickpeas or garbanzo beans, drained, rinsed

1 can (14.5 oz) diced tomatoes and green chiles, undrained

½ cup frozen shelled edamame (soybeans) (from 12-oz bag) or lima beans (from 9-oz bag), thawed

2 tablespoons chopped fresh cilantro

Green bell peppers, halved, if desired

DRESSING

3 tablespoons olive oil

1 teaspoon ground coriander

½ teaspoon ground cumin

½ teaspoon ground cinnamon

1 Cook couscous in water with ¼ teaspoon salt as directed on package.

2 Meanwhile, in medium bowl, mix chickpeas, tomatoes, soybeans and cilantro. In small bowl, mix dressing ingredients until well blended.

3 Add cooked couscous to salad; mix well. Pour dressing over salad; stir gently to mix. Spoon salad mixture into halved bell peppers. Serve immediately, or cover and refrigerate until serving time.

Betty Tip

Edamame is the Japanese name for fresh green soybeans—tasty, bright little green gems that are high in protein. You can buy them frozen, usually in their fuzzy green pods.

1 Serving: Calories 380 (Calories from Fat 130); Total Fat 14g (Saturated Fat 2g; Trans Fat 0g); Cholesterol 0mg; Sodium 290mg; Total Carbohydrate 49g (Dietary Fiber 9g; Sugars 4g); Protein 14g **% Daily Value:** Vitamin A 4%; Vitamin C 10%; Calcium 10%; Iron 30% **Exchanges:** 2½ Starch, ½ Other Carbohydrate, 1 Vegetable, ½ Very Lean Meat, 2½ Fat

Italian Pasta Salad

PREP TIME: **20 MINUTES** • START TO FINISH: **20 MINUTES** • 8 SERVINGS (1 CUP EACH) • *Carbohydrate Choices* 2

6 oz uncooked whole wheat linguine, broken into thirds

¾ cup red wine vinaigrette dressing

¾ teaspoon dried basil leaves

½ teaspoon garlic-pepper blend

3 drops red pepper sauce

½ lb thinly sliced cooked roast beef, cut into strips (2 cups)

1 cup sliced celery (2 medium stalks)

2 medium tomatoes, peeled, seeded and coarsely chopped

1 large cucumber, cut in half lengthwise, thinly sliced

1 jar (4.5 oz) whole mushrooms, drained

1 Cook and drain linguine as directed on package. Rinse with cold water to cool; drain well.

2 Meanwhile, in small bowl, mix dressing, basil, garlic-pepper blend and red pepper sauce until well blended.

3 In large bowl, mix cooked linguine with remaining ingredients. Pour dressing mixture over salad; toss gently to coat. Serve immediately, or cover and refrigerate until serving time.

Betty Tip

Here's a great do-ahead idea for pasta—you can cook the linguine up to 24 hours ahead of assembling the salad. Just cool it, toss it with about 1 tablespoon of canola oil, and store it in a resealable plastic bag in the refrigerator.

1 Serving: Calories 230 (Calories from Fat 80); Total Fat 9g (Saturated Fat 2.5g; Trans Fat 0g); Cholesterol 20mg; Sodium 380mg; Total Carbohydrate 26g (Dietary Fiber 3g; Sugars 9g); Protein 11g
% Daily Value: Vitamin A 8%; Vitamin C 10%; Calcium 2%; Iron 10% **Exchanges:** 1 Starch, ½ Other Carbohydrate, 1 Vegetable, 1 Lean Meat, 1 Fat

Brown Rice–Veggie Salad

PREP TIME: **15 MINUTES** • START TO FINISH: **25 MINUTES** • 4 SERVINGS (1 CUP EACH) • *Carbohydrate Choices* 2½

DRESSING

3 tablespoons reduced-
   sodium soy sauce

1 tablespoon canola oil

1 tablespoon white vinegar

1 teaspoon sugar

SALAD

1½ cups water

1½ cups uncooked instant
   brown rice

1 cup shredded carrots
   (2 medium)

1 cup fresh sugar snap peas,
   strings removed, thinly
   sliced

2 medium green onions, finely
   chopped (2 tablespoons)

1 In small bowl, beat dressing ingredients with wire whisk until smooth; set aside.

2 In 1-quart saucepan, heat water to boiling over high heat. Stir in rice. Heat to boiling. Reduce heat to low; cover and simmer 5 minutes. Remove from heat. Let stand covered 5 minutes. Fluff with fork; cool slightly.

3 In large bowl, toss rice, carrots, peas and onions with dressing. Let stand at room temperature at least 10 minutes to blend flavors.

Betty Tip

This rice-veggie salad can easily be made ahead of time and refrigerated. In fact, doing that not only saves you time later but it also makes the salad more flavorful.

1 Serving: Calories 200 (Calories from Fat 40); Total Fat 5g (Saturated Fat 0g; Trans Fat 0g); Cholesterol 0mg; Sodium 440mg; Total Carbohydrate 38g (Dietary Fiber 2g; Sugars 4g); Protein 4g
% Daily Value: Vitamin A 100%; Vitamin C 20%; Calcium 0%; Iron 4% **Exchanges:** 2 Starch, 1 Fat

White Bean, Herb and Tomato Salad

5 ingredients

PREP TIME: **5 MINUTES** • START TO FINISH: **30 MINUTES** • 7 SERVINGS (½ CUP EACH) • *Carbohydrate Choices* **1**

1 can (19 oz) cannellini (white kidney) beans, drained, rinsed

¾ cup cubed mozzarella cheese

2 tablespoons chopped fresh or 2 teaspoons dried basil leaves

⅓ cup fat-free balsamic vinaigrette

2 medium tomatoes, chopped (1½ cups)

In large bowl, mix all ingredients. Serve immediately, or cover and refrigerate 25 minutes before serving.

Betty Tip

For a little extra flavor, add chopped red onion and a few kalamata olives.

1 Serving: Calories 140 (Calories from Fat 30); Total Fat 3g (Saturated Fat 2g; Trans Fat 0g); Cholesterol 10mg; Sodium 200mg; Total Carbohydrate 18g (Dietary Fiber 4g; Sugars 2g); Protein 10g **% Daily Value:** Vitamin A 8%; Vitamin C 8%; Calcium 15%; Iron 15% **Exchanges:** 1 Starch, 1 Lean Meat

Noodles and Peanut Sauce Salad Bowl

PREP TIME: **25 MINUTES** • START TO FINISH: **25 MINUTES** • 4 SERVINGS (1¾ CUPS EACH) • *Carbohydrate Choices*

8 oz uncooked whole wheat linguine, broken in half

2 cups fresh broccoli florets

1 cup julienne-cut (matchstick-size) carrots (from 10-oz bag)

1 medium bell pepper, cut into bite-size pieces

¼ cup peanut butter

2 tablespoons water

2 teaspoons canola oil

2 tablespoons rice vinegar or white vinegar

2 tablespoons reduced-sodium soy sauce

½ teaspoon ground ginger

⅛ teaspoon ground red pepper (cayenne)

3 medium green onions, chopped (3 tablespoons)

3 tablespoons chopped fresh cilantro

1   Cook linguine as directed on package, adding broccoli, carrots and bell pepper during last minute of cooking; drain pasta and vegetables. Rinse with cold water until pasta and vegetables are cool; drain.

2   Place peanut butter in small bowl. Gradually beat water and oil into peanut butter with wire whisk until smooth. Beat in vinegar, soy sauce, ginger and ground red pepper until blended.

3   In large serving bowl, stir together pasta mixture, peanut sauce, onions and cilantro until well mixed.

Betty Tip

Wow! This recipe is high in iron, vitamins and fiber, and at 3½ carb choices, it's a meal in itself. It's also very colorful, flavorful and great to serve to your family or when entertaining.

1 Serving: Calories 370 (Calories from Fat 100); Total Fat 12g (Saturated Fat 2g; Trans Fat 0g); Cholesterol 0mg; Sodium 570mg; Total Carbohydrate 51g (Dietary Fiber 8g; Sugars 6g); Protein 14g **% Daily Value:** Vitamin A 120%; Vitamin C 60%; Calcium 8%; Iron 15% **Exchanges:** 2½ Starch, ½ Other Carbohydrate, 1 Vegetable, ½ High-Fat Meat, 1½ Fat

Spicy Polenta

PREP TIME: **30 MINUTES** • START TO FINISH: **30 MINUTES** • 4 SERVINGS (¾ CUP EACH) • *Carbohydrate Choices* **2**

3 cups fat-free chicken broth with 33% less sodium or vegetable broth

1 cup fat-free (skim) milk

½ teaspoon ground cumin

¼ teaspoon salt

¼ teaspoon ground red pepper (cayenne)

1 cup uncooked corn grits or coarse-ground cornmeal

¼ cup shredded Parmesan cheese

1 In 3-quart saucepan, heat broth, milk, cumin, salt and red pepper to boiling. Slowly pour grits into boiling broth mixture, stirring vigorously with wire whisk to prevent lumps from forming.

2 Reduce heat to low; simmer uncovered 20 to 25 minutes, stirring occasionally, until thickened. Stir in cheese.

Betty Tip

Serve this tasty polenta with a cool, crisp salad and breadsticks.

1 Serving: Calories 210 (Calories from Fat 18); Total Fat 2.5g (Saturated Fat 1g; Trans Fat 0g); Cholesterol 0mg; Sodium 700mg; Total Carbohydrate 35g (Dietary Fiber 0g; Sugars 5g); Protein 11g **% Daily Value:** Vitamin A 4%; Vitamin C 0%; Calcium 18%; Iron 14% **Exchanges:** 2½ Starch

Lentil-Corn Pilaf

PREP TIME: **10 MINUTES** • START TO FINISH: **30 MINUTES** • 4 SERVINGS (¾ CUP EACH) • *Carbohydrate Choices* 2

2 cups water

1 cup dried lentils (8 oz), sorted, rinsed

½ cup chopped red bell pepper

1 cup frozen (thawed) or canned (drained) whole kernel corn

2 tablespoons chopped fresh cilantro or parsley

½ teaspoon salt

½ teaspoon chili powder

1 In 2-quart saucepan, heat water to boiling. Stir in lentils and bell pepper. Reduce heat; cover and simmer 15 to 20 minutes or until lentils are tender. Drain if necessary.

2 Stir in remaining ingredients. Cook over low heat 2 to 3 minutes, stirring occasionally, until corn is tender and hot.

Betty Tip

For more south-of-the-border spice, chop a jalapeño chile and add with the red bell pepper.

This fiber-rich pilaf makes a terrific accompaniment to grilled pork chops or baked chicken.

1 Serving: Calories 210 (Calories from Fat 0); Total Fat 1g (Saturated Fat 0g; Trans Fat 0g); Cholesterol 0mg; Sodium 300mg; Total Carbohydrate 35g (Dietary Fiber 9g; Sugars 2g); Protein 14g
% Daily Value: Vitamin A 18%; Vitamin C 35%; Calcium 0%; Iron 26% **Exchanges:** 2 Starch, 2 Vegetable, 1 Very Lean Meat

Lentil-Tofu Soup • *Page 173*

Cooking for Two

7

Peppers Stuffed with Broccoli, Beans and Rice

PREP TIME: **20 MINUTES** • START TO FINISH: **30 MINUTES** • 2 SERVINGS • *Carbohydrate Choices* 3

2 large bell peppers, cut in half lengthwise, seeded

⅔ cup water

½ cup uncooked instant brown rice

1 cup chopped fresh broccoli

2 tablespoons chopped onion

½ cup canned red beans, drained, rinsed

⅓ cup chunky-style salsa

¼ cup shredded reduced-fat Cheddar cheese (1 oz)

2 tablespoons chopped fresh cilantro

1 In 8- or 9-inch square microwavable dish, place peppers, cut sides down. Cover dish with plastic wrap, folding back one edge or corner ¼ inch to vent steam. Microwave on High about 4 minutes or until tender.

2 Meanwhile, in 1-quart saucepan, heat water to boiling over high heat. Stir in rice, broccoli and onion. Reduce heat to low; cover and simmer about 10 minutes or until water is absorbed. Stir in beans and salsa.

3 Spoon hot rice mixture into pepper halves. Place filled sides up in microwavable dish. Sprinkle each pepper half with 1 tablespoon of the cheese.

4 Cover dish with plastic wrap, folding back one edge or corner ¼ inch to vent steam. Microwave on High about 1 minute or until cheese is melted. Sprinkle with cilantro. Let stand 1 to 2 minutes before serving.

Betty Tip

Instead of sticking with green, splurge on colorful red, yellow or orange bell peppers. Not only do they retain their color, they add more sweetness than green bell peppers.

1 Serving: Calories 260 (Calories from Fat 20); Total Fat 2.5g (Saturated Fat 1g; Trans Fat 0g); Cholesterol 0mg; Sodium 430mg; Total Carbohydrate 46g (Dietary Fiber 8g; Sugars 7g); Protein 13g **% Daily Value:** Vitamin A 20%; Vitamin C 150%; Calcium 15%; Iron 15% **Exchanges:** 2 Starch, ½ Other Carbohydrate, 2 Vegetable, ½ Lean Meat

Grilled Shrimp Louis Salad

PREP TIME: **25 MINUTES** • START TO FINISH: **25 MINUTES** • 2 SERVINGS • *Carbohydrate Choices* **1**

SALAD

½ lb uncooked deveined peeled medium (31 to 35 count) shrimp, thawed if frozen, tail shells removed

1 teaspoon olive or canola oil

⅛ teaspoon salt

4 cups chopped romaine lettuce

½ cup finely chopped celery (1 medium stalk)

½ cup chopped red bell pepper

1 cup grape tomatoes, cut in half

DRESSING

2 tablespoons reduced-fat mayonnaise or salad dressing

1 tablespoon plain low-fat yogurt

1 tablespoon shrimp cocktail sauce

½ teaspoon grated lemon peel

⅛ teaspoon salt

1 to 2 tablespoons fat-free (skim) milk

1 Heat gas or charcoal grill. On each of 2 (12-inch) metal skewers, thread shrimp, leaving ¼-inch space between each shrimp. Brush with oil. Sprinkle with ⅛ teaspoon salt.

2 Place kabobs on grill over medium heat. Cover grill; cook 4 to 6 minutes, turning once, until shrimp are pink.

3 On 2 serving plates, place lettuce. Top with celery, bell pepper and tomatoes. Remove shrimp from skewers; place over tomatoes.

4 In small bowl, mix all dressing ingredients, adding enough milk for desired consistency. Spoon dressing onto centers of salads.

Betty Tip

Consider serving the dressing on the side so you can determine how much to use on your salad.

A glass of skim milk and Parmesan–Black Pepper Breadsticks (page 22) go nicely with the salad.

1 Serving: Calories 220 (Calories from Fat 80); Total Fat 9g (Saturated Fat 1.5g; Trans Fat 0g); Cholesterol 165mg; Sodium 720mg; Total Carbohydrate 14g (Dietary Fiber 4g; Sugars 9g); Protein 21g **% Daily Value:** Vitamin A 160%; Vitamin C 180%; Calcium 10%; Iron 20% **Exchanges:** 1 Other Carbohydrate, 3 Very Lean Meat, 1½ Fat

Fresh Tomato and Cucumber Salad

PREP TIME: **10 MINUTES** • START TO FINISH: **15 MINUTES** • 2 SERVINGS • *Carbohydrate Choices* ½

1 medium tomato, cut into
   6 slices

½ cup chopped cucumber

⅛ teaspoon salt

1½ teaspoons finely chopped
   fresh basil leaves

1 teaspoon grated lemon peel

1 teaspoon sugar

1 tablespoon balsamic
   vinegar

1   On 2 salad plates, arrange tomato slices in a circle, slightly overlapping. Top with cucumber. Sprinkle salt over tomatoes and cucumber.

2   In small bowl, mix basil, lemon peel and sugar; sprinkle over salads. Drizzle with vinegar. Let stand 5 minutes before serving.

Betty Tip

If you prefer parsley, use it in place of the basil.

For an even more colorful presentation, use 2 small tomatoes, 1 red and 1 yellow, and alternate the slices on the plates.

1 Serving: Calories 30 (Calories from Fat 0); Total Fat 0g (Saturated Fat 0g; Trans Fat 0g); Cholesterol 0mg; Sodium 150mg; Total Carbohydrate 6g (Dietary Fiber 1g; Sugars 5g); Protein 0g **% Daily Value:** Vitamin A 10%; Vitamin C 15%; Calcium 0%; Iron 0% **Exchanges:** 1 Vegetable

Lentil-Tofu Soup

PREP TIME: **30 MINUTES** • START TO FINISH: **30 MINUTES** • 2 SERVINGS (ABOUT 1¼ CUPS EACH) • *Carbohydrate Choices* 2

1 tablespoon canola oil

1 small onion, chopped (¼ cup)

1½ teaspoons curry powder

½ teaspoon ground cumin

1 clove garlic, finely chopped

⅓ cup dried lentils, sorted, rinsed

2½ cups fat-free vegetable broth with ⅓ less sodium (from 32-oz carton)

4 oz firm tofu (from 12-oz package)

¾ cup coarsely chopped fresh broccoli

2 tablespoons chopped fresh parsley

1 In 2-quart saucepan, heat oil over medium heat. Add onion, curry powder, cumin and garlic; cook, stirring occasionally, 4 to 6 minutes or until onion is tender. Stir in lentils and broth. Heat to boiling. Reduce heat; cover and simmer 10 minutes.

2 Meanwhile, cut tofu into ½-inch pieces.

3 Stir tofu, broccoli and parsley into simmering lentil mixture. Cook over medium heat about 5 to 8 minutes, stirring occasionally, until broccoli is crisp-tender.

Betty Tip

This hearty, flavorful soup is a great way to add tofu to your diet. If you'd rather make Lentil-Chicken Soup, just substitute ¾ cup cut-up cooked chicken (about 4 ounces) for the tofu.

1 Serving: Calories 270 (Calories from Fat 90); Total Fat 10g (Saturated Fat 1g; Trans Fat 0g); Cholesterol 0mg; Sodium 370mg; Total Carbohydrate 31g (Dietary Fiber 7g; Sugars 6g); Protein 15g **% Daily Value:** Vitamin A 40%; Vitamin C 35%; Calcium 15%; Iron 30% **Exchanges:** 2 Starch, 1½ Medium-Fat Meat

Caribbean Turkey Stew

PREP TIME: **15 MINUTES** • START TO FINISH: **30 MINUTES** • 2 SERVINGS (1¾ CUPS EACH) • *Carbohydrate Choices*

2 teaspoons olive oil

1 turkey breast tenderloin (½ lb), cut into 1-inch pieces

1 small onion, coarsely chopped (¼ cup)

1 clove garlic, finely chopped

2 small red potatoes, cut into eighths (¾ cup)

½ dark-orange sweet potato, peeled, cut into 1-inch pieces (¾ cup)

1 can (14 oz) chicken broth

¼ teaspoon ground nutmeg

⅛ teaspoon pepper

1 dried bay leaf

½ cup frozen sweet peas, thawed

1   In 3-quart saucepan, heat oil over medium-high heat. Add turkey, onion and garlic; cook 4 to 5 minutes, stirring frequently, until onion is softened.

2   Stir in remaining ingredients except peas. Heat to boiling. Reduce heat to medium-low; cover and cook 15 minutes or until potatoes are tender and turkey is no longer pink in center.

3   Stir in peas. Cover; cook 2 to 3 minutes, stirring occasionally, until peas are hot. Remove bay leaf.

Betty Tip

You can reduce the amount of sodium in this—or any—soup by using reduced-sodium broth.

1 Serving: Calories 390 (Calories from Fat 60); Total Fat 7g (Saturated Fat 1.5g; Trans Fat 0g); Cholesterol 75mg; Sodium 940mg; Total Carbohydrate 47g (Dietary Fiber 7g; Sugars 7g); Protein 35g **% Daily Value:** Vitamin A 170%; Vitamin C 25%; Calcium 8%; Iron 30% **Exchanges:** 2½ Starch, ½ Other Carbohydrate, 4 Very Lean Meat, ½ Fat

Ham and Arugula Open-Face Sandwiches

PREP TIME: 10 MINUTES • START TO FINISH: **10 MINUTES** • 2 SANDWICHES • *Carbohydrate Choices* 1

2 tablespoons reduced-fat mayonnaise or salad dressing

½ teaspoon prepared horseradish

½ teaspoon white wine vinegar or white vinegar

Dash pepper

2 slices whole-grain rye bread

¼ lb thinly sliced cooked ham (from deli)

¼ cup firmly packed arugula or spinach leaves

2 radishes, sliced (2 tablespoons)

1 In small bowl, mix mayonnaise, horseradish, vinegar and pepper. Spread about 1 tablespoon mayonnaise mixture on each bread slice.

2 Layer ham and arugula alternately on bread. Top with radishes.

Betty Tip

This is a terrific sandwich for a light lunch. Team it with any of the soups in this chapter for a heartier meal.

1 Sandwich: Calories 210 (Calories from Fat 80); Total Fat 9g (Saturated Fat 2g; Trans Fat 0g); Cholesterol 35mg; Sodium 1000mg; Total Carbohydrate 18g (Dietary Fiber 1g; Sugars 2g); Protein 15g **% Daily Value:** Vitamin A 0%; Vitamin C 4%; Calcium 4%; Iron 10% **Exchanges:** 1 Starch, 1½ Lean Meat, 1 Fat

Curried Chicken Sandwiches

PREP TIME: **10 MINUTES** • START TO FINISH: **10 MINUTES** • 2 SANDWICHES • *Carbohydrate Choices*

⅔ cup diced cooked chicken

2 tablespoons reduced-fat mayonnaise or salad dressing

2 tablespoons sliced celery

1 tablespoon chopped peanuts

1 tablespoon chutney

½ teaspoon curry powder

2 lettuce leaves

4 slices raisin bread, toasted, if desired

1 In small bowl, mix all ingredients except lettuce and bread.

2 Place lettuce on 2 bread slices. Spoon and spread about ½ cup chicken mixture onto each. Top with remaining bread.

Betty Tip

Any type of chutney works well in this tasty sandwich.

In place of the celery, use any sliced or chopped fresh vegetable you have on hand.

1 Sandwich: Calories 180 (Calories from Fat 100); Total Fat 11g (Saturated Fat 2g; Trans Fat 0g); Cholesterol 45mg; Sodium 170mg; Total Carbohydrate 5g (Dietary Fiber 0g; Sugars 3g); Protein 15g **% Daily Value:** Vitamin A 2%; Vitamin C 2%; Calcium 0%; Iron 4% **Exchanges:** ½ Other Carbohydrate, 2 Lean Meat, 1 Fat

Tex-Mex Veggie Burgers

PREP TIME: **25 MINUTES** • START TO FINISH: **25 MINUTES** • 2 SERVINGS • *Carbohydrate Choices* 3

½ cup frozen whole kernel corn

¼ cup finely chopped red bell pepper

1 tablespoon cider vinegar

¼ teaspoon chili powder

⅛ teaspoon ground cumin

2 frozen soy-protein vegetable burgers

2 whole wheat pita breads (6 inch), cut in half to form pockets

2 tablespoons reduced-fat sour cream

1 Heat gas or charcoal grill. In 1-quart saucepan, mix corn, bell pepper, vinegar, chili powder and cumin. Heat to boiling. Reduce heat to medium-low; cook about 5 minutes or until vegetables are crisp-tender.

2 Place burgers on grill over medium heat. Cover grill; cook 8 to 12 minutes, turning once, until thoroughly heated.

3 Cut burgers in half. Place each burger half in pita bread pocket. Top with corn mixture and sour cream.

Betty Tip

To complete this meal, serve these Tex-Mex burgers with a hearty side salad drizzled with low-fat dressing.

1 Serving: Calories 340 (Calories from Fat 70); Total Fat 8g (Saturated Fat 2.5g; Trans Fat 0g); Cholesterol 10mg; Sodium 700mg; Total Carbohydrate 50g (Dietary Fiber 9g; Sugars 8g); Protein 18g **% Daily Value:** Vitamin A 30%; Vitamin C 35%; Calcium 15%; Iron 20% **Exchanges:** 2½ Starch, 1 Other Carbohydrate, 1½ Lean Meat

Grilled Stuffed Tuna Melts

PREP TIME: **30 MINUTES** • START TO FINISH: **30 MINUTES** • 2 SANDWICHES • *Carbohydrate Choices* 3

1 can (6 oz) water-packed white tuna, drained, rinsed

2 tablespoons finely chopped onion

2 tablespoons finely chopped green bell pepper

1 tablespoon finely chopped dill pickles

2 tablespoons creamy Dijon mustard-mayonnaise spread

¼ cup shredded reduced-fat sharp Cheddar cheese (1 oz)

4 slices whole-grain bread

1 Heat gas or charcoal grill for indirect cooking as directed by manufacturer. Cut 2 (12 × 12-inch) sheets of heavy-duty foil. In small bowl, mix tuna, onion, bell pepper and pickles. Stir in mustard-mayonnaise spread and cheese.

2 Spoon tuna mixture onto 2 bread slices; add remaining bread slices. Cut sandwiches in half. Place 1 whole sandwich on center of 1 foil sheet. Bring up 2 sides of foil over sandwich so edges meet. Seal edges, making tight ½-inch fold; fold again, allowing space for heat circulation and expansion. Fold other sides to seal.

3 Place packets on grill for indirect cooking. Cover grill; cook 12 to 15 minutes, rotating packets ½ turn after 6 minutes, until sandwiches are thoroughly heated. To serve, cut large X across top of each packet; carefully fold back foil to allow steam to escape.

Betty Tip

Add crunch to your lunch! Serve these sandwiches with baby carrots, celery sticks and veggie chips.

The foil-wrapped sandwiches are grilled over indirect heat as direct heat can cause the bread to burn quickly inside the foil.

1 Sandwich: Calories 330 (Calories from Fat 40); Total Fat 4.5g (Saturated Fat 1.5g; Trans Fat 0.5g); Cholesterol 25mg; Sodium 820mg; Total Carbohydrate 44g (Dietary Fiber 6g; Sugars 10g); Protein 28g **% Daily Value:** Vitamin A 0%; Vitamin C 6%; Calcium 10%; Iron 20% **Exchanges:** 2 Starch, 1 Other Carbohydrate, 3 Very Lean Meat

Tuna in Pitas

PREP TIME: **5 MINUTES** • START TO FINISH: **5 MINUTES** • 2 SERVINGS • *Carbohydrate Choices* 1

1 tablespoon finely chopped onion

2 tablespoons finely chopped celery

2 tablespoons reduced-fat mayonnaise or salad dressing

½ teaspoon curry powder

1 can (3 oz) light tuna in water, drained

2 lettuce leaves

1 whole wheat pita bread, cut in half to form 2 pockets

½ medium orange, peeled, broken into segments and cut into ½-inch pieces

1 In small bowl, mix onion, celery, mayonnaise and curry powder. Stir in tuna.

2 Place lettuce leaf in each pita bread half; fill with tuna mixture. Top with orange pieces.

Chicken in Pitas: Use ½ cup cut-up cooked chicken instead of the tuna.

Betty Tip

Then, add a side of plain fat-free yogurt, a few slices of cucumber and a glass of sparkling water for a refreshing lunch.

1 Serving: Calories 180 (Calories from Fat 50); Total Fat 6g (Saturated Fat 1g; Trans Fat 0g); Cholesterol 15mg; Sodium 350mg; Total Carbohydrate 19g (Dietary Fiber 3g; Sugars 6g); Protein 12g
% Daily Value: Vitamin A 4%; Vitamin C 30%; Calcium 2%; Iron 8% **Exchanges:** 1 Starch, 1½ Very Lean Meat, 1 Fat

Pork Tenderloin with Pineapple Salsa

PREP TIME: **25 MINUTES** • START TO FINISH: **25 MINUTES** • 2 SERVINGS • *Carbohydrate Choices*

½ teaspoon finely chopped gingerroot or ¼ teaspoon ground ginger

½ teaspoon salt

¼ teaspoon ground cumin

½ lb pork tenderloin

1 kiwifruit, peeled, chopped

1 (½-inch-thick) slice pineapple, rind removed, cut into ½-inch pieces

1 tablespoon orange marmalade

1 teaspoon finely chopped jalapeño chile

1 Heat gas or charcoal grill. In small bowl, mix gingerroot, salt and cumin. Rub ginger mixture over pork.

2 Place pork on grill over medium heat. Cover grill; cook 15 to 20 minutes, turning occasionally, until pork has slight blush of pink in center and meat thermometer inserted in center reads 160°F.

3 Meanwhile, in small bowl, stir remaining ingredients until marmalade is completely mixed in.

4 Cut pork into thin slices. Serve with pineapple salsa.

Betty Tip

You may have to ask the butcher to cut a ½-pound piece from a larger pork tenderloin for this recipe.

Go flavorful—serve papaya slices on the side to enhance the flavors of the pineapple salsa.

1 Serving: Calories 220 (Calories from Fat 40); Total Fat 4.5g (Saturated Fat 1.5g; Trans Fat 0g); Cholesterol 70mg; Sodium 650mg; Total Carbohydrate 18g (Dietary Fiber 2g; Sugars 12g); Protein 26g **% Daily Value:** Vitamin A 0%; Vitamin C 90%; Calcium 2%; Iron 10% **Exchanges:** 1 Other Carbohydrate, 3½ Very Lean Meat, ½ Fat

Southwest Grilled Pork Chops and Corn

PREP TIME: **30 MINUTES** • START TO FINISH: **30 MINUTES** • 2 SERVINGS • *Carbohydrate Choices*

2 bone-in pork rib chops,
½ inch thick (¾ lb)

3 teaspoons southwestern
seasoning mix

2 tablespoons chopped fresh
cilantro

2 teaspoons butter or
margarine, melted

1 teaspoon lime juice

2 ears frozen corn-on-the-cob

1 Heat gas or charcoal grill for indirect cooking as directed by manufacturer. Sprinkle pork chops with 2 teaspoons of the seasoning mix. Let stand at room temperature no more than 5 minutes.

2 Meanwhile, in small bowl, mix cilantro, melted butter, lime juice and remaining 1 teaspoon seasoning mix. Coat corn with 1 tablespoon cilantro mixture; reserve remaining mixture. Wrap each ear of corn in heavy-duty foil, sealing edges well and leaving room for heat expansion.

3 Place pork on unheated side of two-burner gas grill or over drip pan on charcoal grill. (If using one-burner gas grill, cook over low heat.) Place corn directly over medium heat. Cover grill; cook 10 minutes. Turn pork and corn; cook 7 to 8 minutes longer or until corn is hot, pork is no longer pink and meat thermometer inserted in center of pork reads 160°F. Serve remaining melted butter mixture with corn and pork.

Betty Tip

Can't find southwestern seasoning mix? Use taco seasoning mix instead.

1 Serving: Calories 310 (Calories from Fat 120); Total Fat 13g (Saturated Fat 5g; Trans Fat 0g); Cholesterol 75mg; Sodium 860mg; Total Carbohydrate 22g (Dietary Fiber 3g; Sugars 3g); Protein 25g **% Daily Value:** Vitamin A 8%; Vitamin C 6%; Calcium 0%; Iron 8% **Exchanges:** 1 Starch, ½ Other Carbohydrate, 3 Lean Meat, ½ Fat

Grilled Rosemary Lamb Chops

PREP TIME: **25 MINUTES** • START TO FINISH: **25 MINUTES** • 2 SERVINGS • *Carbohydrate Choices* ½

1 tablespoon country-style
   Dijon mustard

1 tablespoon chopped fresh
   rosemary

2 teaspoons honey

1 clove garlic, finely chopped

½ teaspoon salt

¼ teaspoon coarse ground
   black pepper

6 French-cut baby lamb chops
   (1 to 1¼ inches thick)

1   Heat gas or charcoal grill. In small bowl, mix all ingredients except lamb. Spread mixture on one side of each lamb chop.

2   Place lamb on grill, coated side up, over medium heat. Cover grill; cook 12 to 15 minutes or until thermometer inserted in center reads 145°F.

Betty Tip

French-cut baby lamb chops usually come three to a package and are found in the packaged meat section of the grocery store.

1 Serving: Calories 330 (Calories from Fat 130); Total Fat 14g (Saturated Fat 5g; Trans Fat 0.5g); Cholesterol 140mg; Sodium 880mg; Total Carbohydrate 7g (Dietary Fiber 0g; Sugars 6g); Protein 43g
% Daily Value: Vitamin A 0%; Vitamin C 0%; Calcium 2%; Iron 20% **Exchanges:** ½ Other Carbohydrate, 6 Very Lean Meat, 2 Fat

Buffalo-Style Turkey Tenderloin

PREP TIME: **25 MINUTES** • START TO FINISH: **25 MINUTES** • 2 SERVINGS • *Carbohydrate Choices* **1**

1 teaspoon olive oil

½ lb turkey breast tenderloin

1 cup refrigerated cooked
   new potato wedges (from
   20-oz bag)

1 medium onion, chopped
   (½ cup)

½ medium red bell pepper,
   chopped (½ cup)

2 tablespoons reduced-fat
   blue cheese dressing

1 to 3 teaspoons cayenne
   pepper sauce or Buffalo
   wing sauce

Chopped fresh parsley,
   if desired

1   In 12-inch nonstick skillet, heat oil over medium-low heat. Add turkey; cover and cook 10 minutes, turning after 5 minutes.

2   Add potatoes, onion and bell pepper to turkey. Cook uncovered about 5 minutes longer, stirring occasionally and adding 1 to 2 tablespoons water if needed, until juice of turkey is clear when center of thickest part is cut (170°F) and potatoes are tender.

3   Meanwhile, in small bowl, mix dressing and pepper sauce.

4   Pour sauce over turkey mixture, stirring to coat. Reduce heat to low. Cook uncovered until sauce is thoroughly heated. Sprinkle with parsley.

Betty Tip

The amount of heat and flavor in pepper sauce varies by brand. The original cayenne pepper sauce has a sweet flavor that is perfect for this Buffalo-style entrée.

1 Serving: Calories 230 (Calories from Fat 40); Total Fat 4.5g (Saturated Fat 1g; Trans Fat 0g); Cholesterol 75mg; Sodium 380mg; Total Carbohydrate 18g (Dietary Fiber 3g; Sugars 6g); Protein 29g **% Daily Value:** Vitamin A 20%; Vitamin C 50%; Calcium 4%; Iron 10% **Exchanges:** ½ Starch, ½ Other Carbohydrate, 1 Vegetable, 3½ Very Lean Meat, ½ Fat

Chicken Sesame Stir-Fry

PREP TIME: **20 MINUTES** • START TO FINISH: **20 MINUTES** • 2 SERVINGS • *Carbohydrate Choices* 2

1 cup water

Dash salt

½ cup uncooked instant brown rice

2 tablespoons reduced-sodium soy sauce

1 teaspoon lemon juice

2 teaspoons cornstarch

½ teaspoon toasted sesame oil

1 teaspoon canola oil

½ lb uncooked chicken breast tenders (not breaded), pieces cut in half lengthwise

1½ cups frozen bell pepper and onion stir-fry (from 1-lb bag), thawed, drained

½ teaspoon sesame seed

1   In 1-quart saucepan, heat ⅔ cup of the water and the salt to boiling over high heat. Stir in rice. Reduce heat to low. Cover; simmer about 10 minutes or until water is absorbed. Fluff with fork.

2   Meanwhile, in small bowl, stir remaining ⅓ cup water, the soy sauce, lemon juice, cornstarch and sesame oil; set aside.

3   Heat nonstick wok or 10-inch skillet over medium-high heat. Add canola oil; rotate wok to coat side. Add chicken; cook and stir 2 to 3 minutes. Add stir-fry vegetables; cook and stir 3 to 5 minutes or until chicken is no longer pink in center and vegetables are crisp-tender.

4   Stir soy sauce mixture into chicken mixture; heat to boiling. Cook and stir until sauce is thickened. Sprinkle with sesame seed. Serve with rice.

Betty Tip

Other frozen vegetable combinations can be substituted for the stir-fry vegetables—just throw in your family's favorite.

1 Serving: Calories 300 (Calories from Fat 50); Total Fat 5g (Saturated Fat 0g; Trans Fat 0g); Cholesterol 50mg; Sodium 750mg; Total Carbohydrate 35g (Dietary Fiber 2g; Sugars 5g); Protein 28g **% Daily Value:** Vitamin A 2%; Vitamin C 30%; Calcium 2%; Iron 6% **Exchanges:** 1½ Starch, ½ Other Carbohydrate, 1 Vegetable, 3 Very Lean Meat, ½ Fat

Glazed Lemon Chicken and Rice

PREP TIME: **20 MINUTES** • START TO FINISH: **20 MINUTES** • 2 SERVINGS • *Carbohydrate Choices*

⅓ cup water

1 tablespoon fresh lemon juice

2 teaspoons cornstarch

2 tablespoons honey

1 teaspoon grated lemon peel

¾ cup uncooked instant white rice

¾ cup water

1 teaspoon olive or canola oil

½ lb boneless skinless chicken breasts, cut into 1-inch pieces

½ teaspoon salt

3 green onions, cut into 1-inch pieces

1 small orange bell pepper, cut into 1-inch pieces

1 In 2-cup measuring cup, stir ⅓ cup water, the lemon juice, cornstarch, honey and lemon peel until cornstarch is dissolved; set aside.

2 Cook rice in ¾ cup water as directed on package; keep warm.

3 Meanwhile, in 10-inch nonstick skillet, heat oil over medium-high heat. Add chicken; sprinkle with salt. Cook 2 to 3 minutes, stirring frequently, until chicken is brown. Stir in onions and bell pepper. Cook 2 to 4 minutes, stirring frequently, until chicken is no longer pink in center. Reduce heat to low.

4 Stir lemon juice mixture in measuring cup. Pour into skillet; stir to coat chicken mixture. Cook until slightly thickened. Serve chicken mixture over rice.

Betty Tip

Purchase chicken breast tenders for a quick alternative to boneless skinless chicken breasts.

For an easy extra touch, garnish this entrée with a sprig of parsley and a twist of lemon.

1 Serving: Calories 410 (Calories from Fat 60); Total Fat 6g (Saturated Fat 1.5g; Trans Fat 0g); Cholesterol 70mg; Sodium 660mg; Total Carbohydrate 60g (Dietary Fiber 1g; Sugars 20g); Protein 29g **% Daily Value:** Vitamin A 8%; Vitamin C 60%; Calcium 6%; Iron 15% **Exchanges:** 2½ Starch, 1½ Other Carbohydrate, 3 Very Lean Meat, ½ Fat

Walnut-Coated Walleye

PREP TIME: **20 MINUTES** • START TO FINISH: **20 MINUTES** • 2 SERVINGS • *Carbohydrate Choices*

¾ lb walleye fillets, cut into 2 serving pieces

2 tablespoons all-purpose flour

1 egg or 2 egg whites

1 tablespoon water

¼ cup all-purpose flour

¼ cup finely chopped walnuts

1 tablespoon chopped fresh chives

¼ teaspoon salt

⅛ teaspoon pepper

2 teaspoons canola oil

1 Rinse fish; pat dry with paper towels. Place 2 tablespoons flour on sheet of waxed paper. In shallow dish, beat egg and water with fork or wire whisk until well mixed. In another shallow dish, mix ¼ cup flour, the walnuts, chives, salt and pepper.

2 Coat fish with flour, then dip into egg mixture. Coat both sides with walnut mixture.

3 In 10-inch nonstick skillet, heat oil over medium heat. Add fish; cook 5 to 10 minutes, turning once, until fish flakes easily with fork.

Betty Tip

Coating the fish with walnuts adds flavor and crunch.

Because walnuts are high in fat (a good fat for your heart), they can become rancid easily, so it's a good idea to taste them before using if you've had them for a while.

1 Serving: Calories 420 (Calories from Fat 170); Total Fat 19g (Saturated Fat 2.5g; Trans Fat 0g); Cholesterol 200mg; Sodium 470mg; Total Carbohydrate 20g (Dietary Fiber 2g; Sugars 0g); Protein 41g **% Daily Value:** Vitamin A 6%; Vitamin C 0%; Calcium 6%; Iron 15% **Exchanges:** 1½ Starch, 5 Very Lean Meat, 3 Fat

Baked Sea Bass

PREP TIME: **10 MINUTES** • START TO FINISH: **30 MINUTES** • 2 SERVINGS • *Carbohydrate Choices* **0**

1 medium leek, finely chopped (½ cup)

2 tablespoons dry white wine or nonalcoholic wine

2 teaspoons butter (do not use margarine)

½ teaspoon dried thyme leaves

⅛ teaspoon salt

⅛ teaspoon pepper

¾ lb sea bass fillets, skin removed, cut into 2 serving pieces

1 tablespoon chopped fresh parsley

1   Heat oven to 350°F. In 8-inch nonstick skillet, cook leeks, wine, butter, thyme, salt and pepper over medium heat, stirring occasionally, until leeks are soft.

2   Place fish in ungreased 8-inch square (2-quart) glass baking dish; spoon leek mixture over top of fish.

3   Cover with foil. Bake 15 to 20 minutes or until fish flakes easily with fork. Sprinkle parsley over top of fish.

Betty Tip

For overall good health, try to eat fish at least once a week. With this easy and great-tasting recipe, that goal won't be hard to achieve.

1 Serving: Calories 200 (Calories from Fat 50); Total Fat 6g (Saturated Fat 3g; Trans Fat 0g); Cholesterol 100mg; Sodium 320mg; Total Carbohydrate 4g (Dietary Fiber 0g; Sugars 0g); Protein 33g **% Daily Value:** Vitamin A 15%; Vitamin C 4%; Calcium 4%; Iron 8% **Exchanges:** 4½ Very Lean Meat, 1 Fat

Shrimp Scampi with Rice

PREP TIME: **10 MINUTES** • START TO FINISH: **20 MINUTES** • 2 SERVINGS (1¼ CUPS EACH) • *Carbohydrate Choices* 1½

1 box (10 oz) frozen white & wild rice (with green beans)

1 teaspoon butter or margarine

1 teaspoon olive oil

2 cloves garlic, finely chopped

½ lb uncooked deveined peeled medium (31 to 35 count) shrimp

2 tablespoons dry white wine or chicken broth

1 tablespoon chopped fresh or 1 teaspoon parsley flakes

1 In 2-quart saucepan, make rice as directed on box.

2 In 8-inch skillet, heat butter, oil and garlic over medium-high heat until butter is melted. Add shrimp; cook and stir 3 to 4 minutes or until shrimp are pink. Stir in wine and parsley. Cook 1 minute.

3 To serve, spoon rice onto serving platter; top with shrimp and juices from skillet.

Betty Tip

This scampi dish is high in iron, an important mineral that carries much-needed oxygen throughout your body. To make sure iron is easily absorbed, eat a vitamin C–containing food at the same time, like an orange, a tomato, some bell pepper or any berries.

1 Serving: Calories 250 (Calories from Fat 70); Total Fat 8g (Saturated Fat 2.5g; Trans Fat 0.5g); Cholesterol 165mg; Sodium 830mg; Total Carbohydrate 25g (Dietary Fiber 1g; Sugars 2g); Protein 21g **% Daily Value:** Vitamin A 10%; Vitamin C 6%; Calcium 8%; Iron 30% **Exchanges:** 1½ Starch, 2½ Very Lean Meat, 1 Fat

Summer Harvest Chicken-Potato
Salad · *Page 204*

Traditional Favorites

8

Easy Chili Mole

PREP TIME: **30 MINUTES** • START TO FINISH: **30 MINUTES** • 8 SERVINGS (ABOUT 1 CUP EACH) • *Carbohydrate Choices* **2**

1 lb extra-lean (at least 90%) ground beef

1 medium onion, chopped (½ cup)

1 package (1.25 oz) Tex-Mex chili seasoning mix

1 can (28 oz) diced tomatoes, undrained

1 can (28 oz) crushed tomatoes

1 can (15 oz) spicy chili beans, undrained

1 oz unsweetened baking chocolate, coarsely chopped

8 soft corn tortillas (6 inch)

1 In 4-quart Dutch oven, cook beef and onion over medium heat, stirring occasionally, until beef is brown; drain.

2 Stir in seasoning mix, both tomatoes and beans. Heat to boiling over high heat. Reduce heat to low; cover and cook 15 minutes, stirring occasionally, to blend flavors. Stir in chocolate just until melted. Serve with tortillas.

Betty Tip

Regular chili seasoning mix and 1 teaspoon finely chopped jalapeño chile can be substituted for the Tex-Mex seasoning mix.

For a change, serve with a crisp green salad and warm wedges of cornbread instead of the tortillas.

1 Serving: Calories 270 (Calories from Fat 70); Total Fat 8g (Saturated Fat 3g; Trans Fat 0g); Cholesterol 35mg; Sodium 830mg; Total Carbohydrate 32g (Dietary Fiber 7g; Sugars 7g); Protein 18g **% Daily Value:** Vitamin A 10%; Vitamin C 15%; Calcium 10%; Iron 110% **Exchanges:** 1½ Starch, ½ Other Carbohydrate, 1 Vegetable, 1½ Lean Meat, ½ Fat

Macaroni Goulash

PREP TIME: **25 MINUTES** • START TO FINISH: **25 MINUTES** • 4 SERVINGS (1 CUP EACH) • *Carbohydrate Choices* **3**

1 lb extra-lean (at least 90%) ground beef

1 cup sliced fresh mushrooms (3 oz)

1 medium onion, chopped (½ cup)

1 medium green bell pepper, chopped (1 cup)

1 cup uncooked elbow macaroni (4 oz)

1 can (15 oz) Italian-style tomato sauce

1 can (14.5 oz) Italian-style stewed tomatoes, undrained

1 cup water

1 tablespoon olive or canola oil

2 teaspoons dried basil leaves

½ teaspoon garlic-pepper blend

¼ cup shredded Parmesan cheese (1 oz), if desired

1 In 12-inch nonstick skillet, cook beef, mushrooms and onion over medium-high heat 5 to 7 minutes, stirring frequently, until beef is thoroughly cooked; drain.

2 Stir in remaining ingredients except cheese. Heat to boiling. Reduce heat to medium-low; cover and cook 10 to 12 minutes, stirring frequently to break up tomatoes and keep macaroni from sticking, until macaroni is tender. Sprinkle with cheese.

Betty Tip
You can use all mushrooms or all bell peppers instead of some of each, or omit one or both and add cooked corn or sliced celery instead.

1 Serving: Calories 420 (Calories from Fat 120); Total Fat 14g (Saturated Fat 4.5g; Trans Fat 0.5g); Cholesterol 70mg; Sodium 910mg; Total Carbohydrate 44g (Dietary Fiber 5g; Sugars 13g); Protein 30g **% Daily Value:** Vitamin A 10%; Vitamin C 35%; Calcium 8%; Iron 30% **Exchanges:** 1½ Starch, 1 Other Carbohydrate, 1½ Vegetable, 3 Lean Meat, 1 Fat

Chicken Rigatoni with Broccoli and Peppers

PREP TIME: **10 MINUTES** • START TO FINISH: **30 MINUTES** • 4 SERVINGS (1¾ CUPS EACH) • *Carbohydrate Choices* 3

2½ cups uncooked rigatoni pasta (7 oz)

2 cups chopped fresh broccoli

1 medium red, orange or yellow bell pepper, cut into 1-inch pieces

1 cup cut-up cooked chicken

½ cup reduced-fat Alfredo pasta sauce (from 10-oz container)

¼ cup finely shredded Parmesan cheese (1 oz), if desired

1 Cook pasta as directed on package, adding broccoli and bell pepper for last 2 minutes of cooking. Drain; return to saucepan.

2 Stir in chicken and Alfredo sauce. Cook over low heat about 4 minutes, stirring occasionally, until chicken and sauce are hot. Sprinkle with cheese.

Betty Tip

Any tubular-shaped pasta, such as penne or ziti, will work fine in this dish, and, to make it vegetarian, just omit the chicken and increase the broccoli to 3 cups.

1 Serving: Calories 350 (Calories from Fat 70); Total Fat 7g (Saturated Fat 3g; Trans Fat 0g); Cholesterol 40mg; Sodium 370mg; Total Carbohydrate 49g (Dietary Fiber 4g; Sugars 4g); Protein 21g **% Daily Value:** Vitamin A 25%; Vitamin C 80%; Calcium 10%; Iron 15% **Exchanges:** 2½ Starch, ½ Other Carbohydrate, 1 Vegetable, 1½ Lean Meat, ½ Fat

Chicken Linguine Alfredo

PREP TIME: 30 MINUTES • START TO FINISH: **30 MINUTES** • 6 SERVINGS • *Carbohydrate Choices* **3**

8 oz uncooked linguine

2 teaspoons butter or margarine

2 tablespoons finely chopped shallot

1 clove garlic, finely chopped

1 pint (2 cups) fat-free half-and-half

3 tablespoons all-purpose flour

½ cup reduced-fat sour cream

¼ cup shredded fresh Parmesan cheese

½ teaspoon salt

⅛ teaspoon white pepper

1¼ lb chicken breast strips for stir-fry

1 jar (7 oz) roasted red bell peppers, drained, thinly sliced

⅓ cup shredded Parmesan cheese (1⅓ oz)

2 tablespoons chopped fresh parsley

1 In 4-quart Dutch oven, cook linguine as directed on package. Drain; rinse with hot water. Return to Dutch oven to keep warm.

2 Meanwhile, in 2-quart saucepan, melt butter over medium heat. Add shallot and garlic; cook and stir 1 minute. In medium bowl, beat half-and-half and flour with wire whisk; add to saucepan. Heat to boiling, stirring frequently. Beat in sour cream with wire whisk. Reduce heat to low; cook 1 to 2 minutes or until heated. Remove from heat; stir in ¼ cup cheese, the salt and pepper.

3 Heat 12-inch nonstick skillet over medium-high heat. Add chicken; cook about 5 minutes, stirring frequently, until no longer pink in center.

4 Add chicken, bell peppers and sauce to linguine; stir to mix. Cook over low heat until thoroughly heated. Garnish each serving with cheese and parsley.

Betty Tip
You can still have great flavor without the fat—this delicious Alfredo uses fat-free half-and-half, reduced-fat sour cream and very little butter. Parmesan cheese and roasted red bell peppers boost the flavor.

1 Serving: Calories 430 (Calories from Fat 110); Total Fat 12g (Saturated Fat 6g; Trans Fat 0g); Cholesterol 80mg; Sodium 710mg; Total Carbohydrate 47g (Dietary Fiber 2g; Sugars 8g); Protein 34g **% Daily Value:** Vitamin A 40%; Vitamin C 45%; Calcium 25%; Iron 15% **Exchanges:** 2 Starch, 1 Other Carbohydrate, 4 Very Lean Meat, 1½ Fat

Bow-Ties with Chicken and Asparagus

PREP TIME: **25 MINUTES** • START TO FINISH: **25 MINUTES** • 6 SERVINGS (1½ CUPS EACH) • *Carbohydrate Choices* 2½

4 cups uncooked bow-tie
(farfalle) pasta (8 oz)

1 lb fresh asparagus spears

1 tablespoon canola oil

1 lb boneless skinless chicken
breasts, cut into 1-inch
pieces

1 package (8 oz) sliced fresh
mushrooms (3 cups)

2 cloves garlic, finely chopped

1 cup fat-free chicken broth
with 33% less sodium

1 tablespoon cornstarch

4 medium green onions,
sliced (¼ cup)

2 tablespoons chopped fresh
basil leaves

Salt, if desired

¼ cup finely shredded
Parmesan cheese (1 oz)

1 Cook and drain pasta as directed on package, omitting salt.

2 Meanwhile, break off tough ends of asparagus as far down as stalks
snap easily. Wash asparagus; cut into 1-inch pieces.

3 In 12-inch nonstick skillet, heat oil over medium-high heat.
Add chicken; cook 2 minutes, stirring occasionally. Stir in asparagus,
mushrooms and garlic. Cook 6 to 8 minutes, stirring occasionally, until
chicken is no longer pink in center and vegetables are tender.

4 In small bowl, gradually stir broth into cornstarch. Stir in onions
and basil. Stir cornstarch mixture into chicken mixture. Cook and stir 1
to 2 minutes or until thickened and bubbly. Season with salt. Toss with
pasta. Sprinkle with cheese.

Betty Tip

This light pasta entrée pairs nicely with a glass of crisp white
wine such as Pinot Grigio or Sauvignon Blanc.

1 Serving: Calories 320 (Calories from Fat 60); Total Fat 7g (Saturated Fat 2g; Trans Fat 0g);
Cholesterol 50mg; Sodium 210mg; Total Carbohydrate 37g (Dietary Fiber 3g; Sugars 2g); Protein 27g
% Daily Value: Vitamin A 8%; Vitamin C 4%; Calcium 10%; Iron 20% **Exchanges:** 2 Starch, 1 Vegetable,
2½ Very Lean Meat, 1 Fat

Chicken and Penne Primavera

PREP TIME: **30 MINUTES** • START TO FINISH: **30 MINUTES** • 4 SERVINGS • *Carbohydrate Choices* 2½

1½ cups uncooked penne or mostaccioli pasta (5¼ oz)

2 teaspoons olive oil

1 lb boneless skinless chicken breasts, cut into 1-inch pieces

1 cup sliced zucchini

1 cup sliced yellow summer squash

1 cup cut (2 inch) fresh asparagus spears

½ cup reduced-fat Italian dressing

¼ cup chopped fresh basil leaves

⅓ cup shredded Parmesan cheese (1⅓ oz)

Coarse ground black pepper, if desired

1 Cook and drain pasta as directed on package, omitting salt.

2 Meanwhile, in 4-quart Dutch oven, heat oil over medium-high heat. Add chicken; cook about 5 minutes, stirring occasionally, until brown on outside and no longer pink in center.

3 Stir in zucchini, squash and asparagus. Cook about 5 minutes, stirring occasionally, until vegetables are crisp-tender.

4 Stir pasta into chicken mixture. Stir in dressing and basil; cook until thoroughly heated. Sprinkle with cheese and pepper.

Betty Tip

Primavera is all about vegetables! To save time, you can slice all the vegetables ahead of time and refrigerate up to 3 hours before you use them.

1 Serving: Calories 420 (Calories from Fat 130); Total Fat 15g (Saturated Fat 4g; Trans Fat 0g); Cholesterol 75mg; Sodium 610mg; Total Carbohydrate 37g (Dietary Fiber 3g; Sugars 4g); Protein 36g **% Daily Value:** Vitamin A 15%; Vitamin C 10%; Calcium 15%; Iron 15% **Exchanges:** 1½ Starch, ½ Other Carbohydrate, 1 Vegetable, 4 Very Lean Meat, 2½ Fat

Crispy Chipotle Chicken Strips

PREP TIME: **20 MINUTES** • START TO FINISH: **25 MINUTES** • 4 SERVINGS (4 CHICKEN STRIPS AND 3 TABLESPOONS SAUCE EACH) •
Carbohydrate Choices 1

¼ cup yellow cornmeal

1½ teaspoons chili powder

1 teaspoon garlic salt

1 lb uncooked chicken breast
tenders (not breaded)

Cooking spray

1 can (8 oz) tomato sauce

1 teaspoon ground cumin

½ teaspoon ground coriander

1 chipotle chile in adobo
sauce (from 7-oz can),
finely chopped

1 teaspoon adobo sauce
(from can of chiles)

1 In shallow dish, mix cornmeal, chili powder and garlic salt. Coat chicken well with cornmeal mixture.

2 Generously spray 12-inch skillet with cooking spray; heat skillet over medium heat. Add chicken strips; spray with cooking spray. Cook 4 to 5 minutes, turning once, until golden brown on outside and no longer pink in center.

3 Meanwhile, in 1-quart saucepan, heat remaining ingredients over medium heat 3 to 4 minutes, stirring occasionally, until hot.

4 Serve chicken with sauce.

Betty Tip

Now you can make your own version of a popular flavorful restaurant dish at home, and with fewer calories and much less fat.

1 Serving: Calories 170 (Calories from Fat 20); Total Fat 2g (Saturated Fat 0g; Trans Fat 0g); Cholesterol 50mg; Sodium 730mg; Total Carbohydrate 13g (Dietary Fiber 2g; Sugars 3g); Protein 26g **% Daily Value:** Vitamin A 10%; Vitamin C 4%; Calcium 0%; Iron 8% **Exchanges:** 1 Starch, 3 Very Lean Meat

Summer Harvest Chicken-Potato Salad

PREP TIME: **15 MINUTES** • START TO FINISH: **30 MINUTES** • 4 SERVINGS • *Carbohydrate Choices* **2**

4 medium red potatoes (1 lb),
cut into ¾-inch cubes

½ lb fresh green beans,
trimmed, cut into 1-inch
pieces (about 2 cups)

½ cup plain fat-free yogurt

⅓ cup fat-free ranch dressing

1 tablespoon prepared
horseradish

¼ teaspoon salt

Dash pepper

2 cups cut-up cooked chicken
breast

⅔ cup thinly sliced celery

Torn salad greens, if desired

1 In 2-quart saucepan, heat 6 cups lightly salted water to boiling. Add potatoes; return to boiling. Reduce heat; simmer 5 minutes. Add green beans; cook uncovered 8 to 12 minutes longer or until potatoes and beans are crisp-tender.

2 Meanwhile, in small bowl, mix yogurt, dressing, horseradish, salt and pepper; set aside.

3 Drain potatoes and green beans; rinse with cold water to cool. In large serving bowl, mix potatoes, green beans, chicken and celery. Pour yogurt mixture over salad; toss gently to coat. Line plates with greens; spoon salad onto greens.

Betty Tip

Not only is this a great-tasting, low-fat comfort food, the potatoes, green beans and celery are an excellent source of fiber. When you eat these foods together, the fiber really adds up!

1 Serving: Calories 270 (Calories from Fat 35); Total Fat 3.5g (Saturated Fat 1g; Trans Fat 0g); Cholesterol 60mg; Sodium 410mg; Total Carbohydrate 32g (Dietary Fiber 5g; Sugars 6g); Protein 26g **% Daily Value:** Vitamin A 10%; Vitamin C 20%; Calcium 15%; Iron 20% **Exchanges:** 1½ Starch, ½ Other Carbohydrate, 1 Vegetable, 2½ Very Lean Meat

Turkey Chef Salad

PREP TIME: **15 MINUTES** • START TO FINISH: **15 MINUTES** • 4 SERVINGS • *Carbohydrate Choices* 2

8 cups bite-size pieces mixed salad greens

1 piece (½ lb) cooked low-sodium turkey (from deli), cut into ¼-inch julienne strips

1 can (15 oz) garbanzo beans, drained, rinsed

1 piece (4 oz) mozzarella cheese, cut into ½-inch cubes

8 radishes, sliced

2 tablespoons balsamic vinegar

4 teaspoons olive or canola oil

½ teaspoon grated lemon peel

½ teaspoon sugar

1 Among 4 dinner plates, divide salad greens. Top evenly with turkey, beans, cheese and radishes.

2 In small bowl, beat remaining ingredients with wire whisk until blended. Drizzle dressing over salads.

Betty Tip

To save time, ask for the ½ pound of low-sodium turkey to be cut into ¼-inch-thick slices. Then you can just cut the large slices into ¼-inch-wide strips.

1 Serving: Calories 360 (Calories from Fat 120); Total Fat 13g (Saturated Fat 4.5g; Trans Fat 0g); Cholesterol 40mg; Sodium 530mg; Total Carbohydrate 31g (Dietary Fiber 8g; Sugars 3g); Protein 29g **% Daily Value:** Vitamin A 110%; Vitamin C 35%; Calcium 30%; Iron 25% **Exchanges:** 1½ Starch, 1½ Vegetable, 3 Very Lean Meat, 2 Fat

Broccoli-Cheese Soup

PREP TIME: **25 MINUTES** • START TO FINISH: **25 MINUTES** • 6 SERVINGS (1 CUP EACH) • *Carbohydrate Choices* **1**

1 tablespoon canola or
   soybean oil

1 medium onion, chopped
   (½ cup)

1 tablespoon all-purpose flour

1 teaspoon salt

3 cups original-flavored
   soymilk or fat-free (skim)
   milk

2 teaspoons cornstarch

1½ cups shredded reduced-
   fat sharp Cheddar cheese
   (6 oz)

3 cups bite-size fresh or
   frozen (thawed) broccoli
   florets

1 cup popped reduced-fat
   popcorn, if desired

1 In 3-quart saucepan, heat oil over medium heat. Stir in onion, flour and salt. Cook 2 to 3 minutes, stirring constantly, until onion is soft.

2 In small bowl, stir soymilk and cornstarch with wire whisk until smooth. Gradually stir into onion mixture. Cook 5 to 6 minutes, stirring frequently, until thick and bubbly.

3 Stir in cheese. Cook about 3 minutes, stirring frequently, until cheese is melted. Stir in broccoli. Cook about 1 minute or until hot, stirring occasionally. Serve topped with popcorn.

Betty Tip

Soy protein, in the context of a low-fat, low-cholesterol diet, can help reduce the risk of heart disease. Research suggests that when about 25 grams of soy protein is eaten daily from soy foods, blood cholesterol levels tend to drop. This yummy soup is a great start, containing about one-third of the 25 daily grams in one serving.

1 Serving: Calories 140 (Calories from Fat 50); Total Fat 6g (Saturated Fat 1.5g; Trans Fat 0g); Cholesterol 5mg; Sodium 760mg; Total Carbohydrate 11g (Dietary Fiber 1g; Sugars 6g); Protein 11g **% Daily Value:** Vitamin A 10%; Vitamin C 35%; Calcium 40%; Iron 6% **Exchanges:** ½ Skim Milk, 1 Vegetable, 1 Medium-Fat Meat

Turkey–Wild Rice Soup

PREP TIME: **10 MINUTES** • START TO FINISH: **30 MINUTES** • 6 SERVINGS (1½ CUPS EACH) • *Carbohydrate Choices* 2

2 tablespoons butter or margarine

½ cup all-purpose flour

2 cans (14 oz each) fat-free chicken broth with 33% less sodium

1 package (8 oz) 98% fat-free oven-roasted turkey breast, cubed (about 2 cups)

2 cups water

2 tablespoons dried chopped onion

1 package (6 oz) original-flavor long-grain and wild rice mix

2 cups original-flavored soymilk or fat-free (skim) milk

1 In 5-quart Dutch oven, melt butter over medium heat. Stir in flour with wire whisk until well blended. Slowly stir in broth with wire whisk.

2 Stir in turkey, water, onion, rice and contents of seasoning packet. Heat to boiling over high heat, stirring occasionally. Reduce heat to medium-low; cover and simmer about 25 minutes or until rice is tender.

3 Stir in soymilk; heat just to boiling.

Betty Tip

Wild rice is really the seed of an aquatic grass. Whatever you want to call it, the wild rice adds a delicious nutty flavor and slightly chewy texture to this quick and tasty soup.

1 Serving: Calories 260 (Calories from Fat 50); Total Fat 6g (Saturated Fat 3g; Trans Fat 0g); Cholesterol 45mg; Sodium 720mg; Total Carbohydrate 33g (Dietary Fiber 0g; Sugars 4g); Protein 19g **% Daily Value:** Vitamin A 6%; Vitamin C 0%; Calcium 15%; Iron 15% **Exchanges:** 1½ Starch, ½ Other Carbohydrate, 2 Very Lean Meat, 1 Fat

Five-Layer Salad

PREP TIME: **10 MINUTES** • START TO FINISH: **25 MINUTES** • 4 SERVINGS (1¹/₃ CUP EACH) • *Carbohydrate Choices* **1**

1 cup frozen sweet peas

1 tablespoon water

¹/₃ cup plain fat-free yogurt

¼ cup reduced-fat mayonnaise (do not use salad dressing)

1 tablespoon cider vinegar

2 teaspoons sugar

½ teaspoon salt

3 cups (from 16-oz bag) coleslaw mix (shredded cabbage and carrots)

1 cup shredded carrots (2 medium)

1 cup halved cherry tomatoes

1 In small microwavable bowl, place peas and water. Cover with microwavable plastic wrap, folding back one edge ¼ inch to vent steam. Microwave on High 4 to 6 minutes, stirring after 2 minutes, until tender; drain. Let stand until cool.

2 Meanwhile, in small bowl, mix yogurt, mayonnaise, vinegar, sugar and salt.

3 In 1½- or 2-quart glass bowl, layer coleslaw mix, carrots, tomatoes and peas. Spread mayonnaise mixture over top. Refrigerate 15 minutes. Toss gently before serving.

Betty Tip

For a complete light meal in a bowl, place 1½ cups chopped cooked chicken between the carrots and tomatoes—it's a six-layer salad.

1 Serving: Calories 140 (Calories from Fat 50); Total Fat 5g (Saturated Fat 0g; Trans Fat 0g); Cholesterol 0mg; Sodium 480mg; Total Carbohydrate 18g (Dietary Fiber 4g; Sugars 10g); Protein 4g
% Daily Value: Vitamin A 160%; Vitamin C 40%; Calcium 8%; Iron 4% **Exchanges:** 1 Other Carbohydrate, 2 Vegetable, 1 Fat

Pesto Pasta Salad

PREP TIME: **15 MINUTES** • START TO FINISH: **30 MINUTES** • 6 SERVINGS (ABOUT 2 CUPS EACH) • *Carbohydrate Choices* 2½

2½ cups uncooked penne pasta (7½ oz)

2 cups bite-size pieces fresh green beans

1 tablespoon pine nuts

1½ cups firmly packed fresh basil leaves

⅓ cup freshly grated Parmesan cheese

1 tablespoon fat-free ricotta cheese

1 clove garlic

¼ cup fat-free chicken broth with 33% less sodium

4 teaspoons extra-virgin olive oil

4 cups washed fresh baby spinach leaves

1 pint (2 cups) cherry tomatoes, halved

¼ cup red wine vinegar

1   Cook pasta as directed on package, omitting salt and adding green beans for last 4 minutes of cooking. Drain pasta, reserving ¼ cup cooking water.

2   Meanwhile, in blender or food processor, place nuts, basil, Parmesan cheese, ricotta cheese, garlic, broth and oil. Cover; blend on medium speed about 3 minutes, stopping occasionally to scrape sides, until smooth.

3   In large bowl, mix pasta, green beans, spinach and tomatoes. Add pesto, vinegar and reserved ¼ cup cooking water; toss to coat.

Betty Tip

This is a great meatless main dish, but if you like, stir in 1½ cups of shredded cooked chicken or a 7-ounce can of tuna, drained and flaked.

Try arugula or field greens instead of the spinach, or chopped cooked broccoli or cauliflower instead of the green beans.

1 Serving: Calories 250 (Calories from Fat 60); Total Fat 7g (Saturated Fat 2g; Trans Fat 0g); Cholesterol 0mg; Sodium 150mg; Total Carbohydrate 37g (Dietary Fiber 4g; Sugars 4g); Protein 11g **% Daily Value:** Vitamin A 60%; Vitamin C 35%; Calcium 15%; Iron 15% **Exchanges:** 2 Starch, 1 Vegetable, ½ Medium-Fat Meat, ½ Fat

Fettuccine and Vegetables Parmesan

PREP TIME: **15 MINUTES** • START TO FINISH: **30 MINUTES** • 4 SERVINGS (1½ CUPS EACH) • *Carbohydrate Choices* 3½

8 oz uncooked fettuccine or linguine

1 cup fresh broccoli florets

1 cup fresh cauliflower florets

1 cup frozen sweet peas, rinsed to separate

2 medium carrots, thinly sliced (1 cup)

1 small onion, chopped (¼ cup)

1 tablespoon butter or stick margarine

¾ cup evaporated fat-free milk (from 12-oz can)

⅓ cup grated Parmesan cheese

½ teaspoon garlic salt

⅛ teaspoon ground nutmeg, if desired

Dash pepper

1 Cook fettuccine as directed on package, omitting salt and adding broccoli, cauliflower, peas, carrots and onion for last 3 minutes of cooking. Drain; return to saucepan and keep warm.

2 Meanwhile, in 10-inch skillet, heat butter and milk over medium heat, stirring frequently, until butter is melted and mixture starts to bubble. Reduce heat to low. Simmer uncovered 3 to 4 minutes, stirring frequently, until slightly thickened. Remove from heat. Stir in cheese, garlic salt, nutmeg and pepper.

3 Stir cheese mixture into pasta mixture.

Betty Tip

Serve a salad of sliced fresh tomatoes drizzled with fat-free balsamic vinaigrette for a colorful, meatless meal.

1 Serving: Calories 370 (Calories from Fat 80); Total Fat 9g (Saturated Fat 4g; Trans Fat 0g); Cholesterol 60mg; Sodium 410mg; Total Carbohydrate 55g (Dietary Fiber 5g; Sugars 11g); Protein 17g
% Daily Value: Vitamin A 130%; Vitamin C 30%; Calcium 30%; Iron 20% **Exchanges:** 2 Starch, 1 Other Carbohydrate, 2 Vegetable, 1 Lean Meat, 1 Fat

Sweet and Spicy Coleslaw

PREP TIME: **10 MINUTES** • START TO FINISH: **25 MINUTES** • 4 SERVINGS (¾ CUP EACH) • *Carbohydrate Choices* 1

4 cups broccoli slaw (from 1-lb bag)

1 medium Red Delicious apple, chopped (1 cup)

⅓ cup plain fat-free yogurt

¼ cup reduced-fat mayonnaise or salad dressing

2 tablespoons sugar

¼ teaspoon original salt-free seasoning blend

¼ teaspoon red pepper sauce

1   In large bowl, mix broccoli slaw and apple.

2   In small bowl, mix remaining ingredients. Stir into broccoli mixture until well mixed. Cover; refrigerate 15 minutes before serving.

Betty Tip

Looking for a spin on an all-time favorite to bring to the next party? This recipe can easily be doubled, and it can be made 1 to 2 hours ahead and chilled.

The broccoli slaw in this recipe is a great source of vitamin C and folic acid.

1 Serving: Calories 135 (Calories from Fat 45); Total Fat 5g (Saturated Fat 1g; Trans Fat 0g); Cholesterol 0mg; Sodium 150mg; Total Carbohydrate 20g (Dietary Fiber 3g; Sugars 14g); Protein 5g
% Daily Value: Vitamin A 12%; Vitamin C 135%; Calcium 12%; Iron 4% **Exchanges:** 1 Other Carbohydrate, 1 Vegetable, 1 Fat

Holidays or Gatherings

Diabetes doesn't take a break just because there's a holiday or family gathering. At a special family dinner or party, maybe you feel like having an extra serving or more dessert than usual. That's okay, just get back on your plan the next day. The key is to find foods you love that fit into your food plan and help you stay on your plan as much as possible.

Here are a few ideas that might help:

1. **Take care of yourself:** Keep yourself hydrated, get enough rest and don't skip meals. You'll be less tempted to overindulge if you keep up your daily health habits.

2. **Plan ahead:** Give up a dinner roll or a helping of potatoes if what you really want is a serving of pumpkin pie. That way, you can still stick to your food plan.

3. **Keep up your daily walk** or other exercise to help keep blood glucose levels down. Have a buddy or family member join you on a walk or other activity.

4. **Keep portion sizes small.** If cheesecake or chocolate is something you just love, have a small wedge or treat and really savor it. This can prevent you from overeating.

5. **Use lower-fat, delicious recipes.** Bake a lower-fat version of a popular pie, quick bread, dessert or snack. For healthy recipe ideas, go to *BettyCrocker*.com and search healthy recipes.

6. **Choose a fun activity** that takes your mind off eating. Try ice-skating, tree-trimming, hosting a party around an active game or sport. Play charades, badminton, croquet, kick a soccer ball, shoot a few hoops—the more active you are, the better.

7. **Bring a dish that fits your food plan.** If you're taking food to a potluck dinner, make sure it's something you can eat. Check out the Traditional Favorites chapter of this book for ideas.

8. **Bring or eat extra veggies** like baby-cut carrots, edamame (soybeans), sliced bell peppers, celery or other low-calorie or free foods to snack on (e.g., popcorn and pretzels).

9. **Drink lots of water.** Jazz up your water by mixing it with a bit of juice or a lemon twist, or buy flavored water to sip on. Homemade hot or iced herb tea without added sugar is also a great, no-cal beverage.

10. **Instead of eating dessert with dinner, eat it as a snack later.** That puts less of a load on your insulin supply than eating it all at one time.

A 10-Day Diabetes Menu Plan

DAY 1

BREAKFAST
1 serving Cheerios® cereal
1 cup fat-free (skim) milk
1 medium banana or ½ cup blueberries
1 cup Spiced-Up Café Latte (page 16),
coffee or herbal tea
265 | 4

SNACK
3 graham crackers
12 sweet cherries
130 | 2

LUNCH
1 serving Rio Grande Turkey Soup (page 43)
1 slice whole wheat bread or dinner roll
1 teaspoon squeeze or soft-tub margarine
Carrot and celery sticks
2 tablespoons reduced-fat vegetable or
ranch dip
1 medium nectarine
500 | 4

DINNER
1 serving Apple-Rosemary Pork and
Barley (page 142)
1 serving Roasted Sesame Asparagus
(page 80) or 1 cup steamed green beans
1 small whole-grain dinner roll
1 teaspoon squeeze or soft-tub margarine
½ cup any flavor sherbet
½ cup cantaloupe or watermelon chunks
1 cup fat-free (skim) milk
600 | 4

SNACK*
1 medium orange or clementine
1 container (6 ounces) low-fat yogurt or ½
cup sugar-free, fat-free chocolate pudding
made with fat-free (skim) milk
2 tablespoons fat-free whipped topping
300 | 3

TOTAL
Calories: 1,700 • Total Fat g: 43g
Sat Fat g: 12g • Carbohydrate Choices: 18
Fiber g: 33g

DAY 2

BREAKFAST
1 Apple-Honey On-the-Go Bar (page 35)
1 cup fat-free (skim) milk
½ cup orange juice
330 | 4

SNACK
1 cup mango chunks
100 | 2

LUNCH
1 serving Cucumber-Tuna Salad
Pitas (page 54)
1 cup grapes
½ cup bell pepper strips or
cucumber slices
1 cup fat-free (skim) milk
360 | 4

DINNER
1 serving Szechuan Beef and
Bean Sprouts (page 118)
1 serving Blueberry and Orange Spinach
Salad (page 75) or mixed-greens salad with
2 tablespoons reduced-fat Caesar dressing
1 small serving lemon or
fudge pudding cake
1 cup fat-free (skim) milk
520 | 4

SNACK*
1 serving Cranberry–Chocolate Chex®
Snack Mix (page 34)
1 medium apple
150 | 2

TOTAL
Calories: 1,450 • Total Fat g: 7g
Sat Fat g: 7g • Carbohydrate Choices: 16
Fiber g: 21g

DAY 3

BREAKFAST
1 Cheerios®-Yogurt-Fruit Parfait (page 20)
290 | 3.5

SNACK
1 small muffin (1½ ounces)
190 | 2

LUNCH
1 serving Spinach-Shrimp Pizza (page 147)
½ cup baby-cut carrots
½ cup pineapple chunks
364 | 3.5

DINNER
1 serving Glazed Lemon Chicken
and Rice (page 188)
1 serving Spicy Green Beans with
Caramelized Onions (page 81)
1 cup fat-free (skim) milk
600 | 5

SNACK*
1 medium pear
3 cups plain popcorn or low-fat
microwave popcorn
1 cup fat-free (skim) milk
270 | 3.5

TOTAL
Calories: 1,760 • Total Fat g: 45g
Sat Fat g: 15g • Carbohydrate Choices:
17.5 • Fiber g: 27g

600 Calories | 4 Carbohydrate Choices

DAY 4

BREAKFAST
1 serving Bacon and Tomato Frittata (page 112)
2 slices whole wheat bread, toasted
2 teaspoons jam or jelly
½ cup cranberry juice

432 | 4

SNACK
½ bagel
1 tablespoon reduced-fat cream cheese

170 | 2

LUNCH
1 serving Lentil-Tofu Soup (page 173)
1 Parmesan–Black Pepper Breadstick (page 22)
1 cup baby-cut carrots
1 medium banana
1 cup fat-free (skim) milk

480 | 4

DINNER
1 serving Tex-Mex Veggie Burgers (page 178)
1 serving Better Than Mashed Potatoes (page 86)
1 small kiwifruit
1 chocolate bar (½ ounce)

500 | 5

SNACK*
2 small molasses cookies or gingersnaps
1 cup fat-free (skim) milk or 1 cup herb tea

180 | 2

TOTAL
Calories: 1,762 • Total Fat g: 58g
Sat Fat g: 20g • Carbohydrate Choices: 17
Fiber g: 32g

DAY 5

BREAKFAST
1 Strawberry-Watermelon-Pomegranate Smoothie (page 18)
1 whole-wheat English muffin
2 teaspoons peanut butter

350 | 4

SNACK
1 whole-grain granola bar

95 | 1

LUNCH
1 serving Trail Mix Chicken Salad (page 67)
1 serving Pear-Ginger Scones (page 21)
1 cup fat-free (skim) milk

580 | 4.5

DINNER
1 serving Quick Taco Skillet Casserole (page 91)
1 serving salad greens with fat-free ranch dressing
1 serving Roasted Bell Pepper Medley (page 87)
1 serving Melon and Grape Salad (page 76)

446 | 4.5

SNACK*
1 serving Three-Cheese and Bacon Spread (page 24)
1 cup fat-free (skim) milk or chocolate skim milk

180 | 2

TOTAL
Calories: 1,650 • Total Fat g: 40g
Sat Fat g: 12g • Carbohydrate Choices: 16 • Fiber g: 23g

DAY 6

BREAKFAST
1 serving old-fashioned or quick-cooking oatmeal
⅓ cup raisins, ½ cup cherries or 1 medium banana
1 cup green tea

290 | 4

SNACK
1 serving Baked Coconut Shrimp (page 36)

130 | 1

LUNCH
1 serving Grilled Stuffed Tuna Melts (page 179)
1 serving Asian Tossed Salad (page 70) or Asparagus-Pepper Stir-Fry (page 78)
1 cup soymilk or fat-free (skim) milk

560 | 3.5

DINNER
1 serving Walnut-Crusted Salmon (page 135)
1 serving Cranberry–Pine Nut Quinoa (page 148)
1 serving Lemon-Garlic Broccoli with Yellow Peppers (page 83)
1 cup fat-free (skim) milk or water

625 | 4

SNACK*
1 serving Creamy Cottage Cheese with Cucumbers (page 31)
2 tablespoons sunflower nuts

210 | 1

TOTAL
Calories: 1,815 • Total Fat g: 70g
Sat Fat g: 17g • Carbohydrate Choices: 13.5 • Fiber g: 25g

SNACK* = eat anytime during the day

A 10-Day Diabetes Menu Plan

DAY 7

BREAKFAST
½ cup high-fiber cereal
1 cup fat-free (skim) milk
1 cup fresh raspberries or blueberries

206 · **3.5**

SNACK
1 serving Pitas with Hummus-Olive Spread (page 23) or 1 whole-grain granola bar
½ cup apple juice or apple cider

228 · **3**

LUNCH
1 serving Chunky Vegetable Chowder (page 47)
6 whole-grain crackers with 1 to 2 ounces mozzarella cheese
1 cup cherry or grape tomatoes
1 cup fat-free (skim) milk

515 · **5.5**

DINNER
1 serving Apricot-Almond Chicken (page 129)
1 serving Quinoa with Black Beans (page 150)
1 serving Broccoli, Pepper and Bacon Toss (page 82)
2 macaroon cookies or 1 slice angel food cake with 2 tablespoons fat-free whipped topping
1 cup hot herbal tea or coffee

600 · **6**

SNACK*
½ cup reduced-fat frozen yogurt or ice cream
1 tablespoon fat-free chocolate fudge topping

180 · **2**

TOTAL
**Calories: 1,730 • Total Fat g: 39g
Sat Fat g: 12g • Carbohydrate Choices: 20
Fiber g: 45g**

DAY 8

BREAKFAST
1 serving Creamy Apple-Cinnamon Quesadilla (page 32)
1 cup fat-free (skim) milk
1 medium orange

250 · **3**

SNACK
1 serving Caramelized Onion–Shrimp Spread (page 26)
1 medium plum or ½ mango chunks

184 · **2**

LUNCH
1 serving Caribbean Turkey Stew (page 174)
1 Parmesan–Black Pepper Breadstick (page 22) or 1 slice whole-wheat bread or 1 small dinner roll or 4 reduced-fat wheat crackers
1 teaspoon squeeze or soft-tub margarine
Bell pepper strips, jicama sticks, or carrot and celery sticks
1 glass water

530 · **4.5**

DINNER
1 serving Seafood and Vegetables with Rice (page 106)
1 serving Blueberry and Orange Spinach Salad (page 75)
1 cup fat-free (skim) milk

430 · **4**

SNACK*
1 serving Ginger and Mint Dip with Fruit (page 27)
1 glass sugar-free iced tea

100 · **1.5**

TOTAL
**Calories: 1,500 • Total Fat g: 30g
Sat Fat g: 8g • Carbohydrate Choices: 15
Fiber g: 22g**

DAY 9

BREAKFAST
1 Raspberry-Banana-Yogurt Smoothie (page 19)

180 · **2**

SNACK
1 serving Spicy Cajun Onion Dip (page 30)

108 · **1**

LUNCH
1 Ultimate California Crab Wrap (page 57)
1 cup grapes
½ cup tomato and cucumber slices
1 cup fat-free (skim) milk

430 · **4**

DINNER
1 serving Curried Turkey Stir-Fry (page 96)
1 serving Asian Tossed Salad (page 70)
1 cup reduced-fat vanilla soymilk or fat-free (skim) milk

650 · **4**

SNACK*
½ cup watermelon or honeydew melon chunks
1 small chocolate cupcake
4 whole-grain crackers

200 · **3**

TOTAL
**Calories: 1,570 • Total Fat g: 50g
Sat Fat g: 15g • Carbohydrate Choices: 14
Fiber g: 25g**

600 Calories **4** Carbohydrate Choices

DAY 10

1 serving Oatmeal Crisp® cereal
½ cup sliced strawberries or raspberries
1 cup fat-free yogurt (any flavor)

440   4

1 Apple-Honey On-the-Go Bar (page 35)
1 serving Spiced-Up Café Latte (page 16)

212   2

1 serving White Bean, Herb and Tomato
Salad (page 161)
1 Parmesan–Black Pepper Breadstick
(page 22) or 1 slice whole wheat bread
1 teaspoon squeeze or soft-tub margarine
½ cup pineapple chunks
1 raspberry-chocolate snack bar
1 cup fat-free (skim) milk

436   4

1 serving Mediterranean Shrimp with
Bulgur (page 100)
1 serving Roasted Asparagus and
Strawberry Salad (page 77)
½ cup steamed edamame (soybeans), corn
or peas

442   4

1 serving Creamy Cottage Cheese with
Cucumbers (page 31)
1 cup soymilk or fat-free (skim) milk

202   1

**Calories: 1,790 • Total Fat g: 44.5g
Sat Fat g: 10.5g • Carbohydrate Choices:
15 • Fiber g: 40g**

SNACK* = eat anytime during the day

Additional Resources

OVERALL HEALTH

Centers for Disease Control and
Prevention
www.cdc.gov
Mayo Clinic
www.mayoclinic.com
U.S. Department of Health & Human
Services
www.hhs.gov

DIABETES

American Diabetes Association
www.diabetes.org or call 1-800-342-2383
American Association of Diabetes
Educators
www.aadenet.org or call 1-800-338-3633
International Diabetes Center
www.internationaldiabetescenter.com
Juvenile Diabetes Research Foundation
International
www.jdrf.org or call 1-800-533-CURE
Children with Diabetes
www.childrenwithdiabetes.com

FITNESS

RECREATION.gov
www.recreation.gov
Melpomene Institute for Women's
Health Research
www.melpomene.org
The President's Council on Physical
Fitness and Sports
www.fitness.gov

HEART HEALTH

American College of Cardiology
www.acc.org
American Heart Association
www.americanheart.org
National Heart, Lung, and Blood Institute
www.nhlbi.nih.gov
Texas Heart Institute
www.texasheartinstitute.org
WomenHeart: The National Coalition
for Women with Heart Disease
www.womenheart.org

NUTRITION AND
HEALTHY EATING

American Dietetic Association
www.eatright.org or call 1-800-877-1600
Consumer Corner, U.S. Department
of Agriculture Food and Nutrition
Information Center
www.nal.usda.gov/fnic/consumersite
International Food Information Council
www.ific.org
MyPyramid.gov, U.S. Department of
Agriculture
www.mypyramid.gov
Type 1 Tools—a catalog with tools to
simplify everyday tasks
www.type1tools.com

WEIGHT MANAGEMENT

WIN: Weight-control Information Network
http://win.niddk.nih.gov
eatbetteramerica™—General Mills
www.eatbetteramerica.com

Helpful Nutrition and Cooking Information

Nutrition Guidelines

We provide nutrition information for each recipe that includes calories, fat, cholesterol, sodium, carbohydrate, fiber and protein. Individual food choices can be based on this information.

Recommended intake for a daily diet of 2,000 calories as set by the Food and Drug Administration

Total Fat	Less than 65g
Saturated Fat	Less than 20g
Cholesterol	Less than 300mg
Sodium	Less than 2,400mg
Total Carbohydrate	300g
Dietary Fiber	25g

Criteria Used for Calculating Nutrition Information

- The first ingredient was used wherever a choice is given (such as 1/3 cup sour cream or plain yogurt).

- The first ingredient amount was used wherever a range is given (such as 3- to 3-1/2–pound cut-up broiler-fryer chicken).

- The first serving number was used wherever a range is given (such as 4 to 6 servings).

- "If desired" ingredients and recipe variations were not included (such as sprinkle with brown sugar, if desired).

- Only the amount of a marinade or frying oil that is estimated to be absorbed by the food during preparation or cooking was calculated.

Ingredients Used in Recipe Testing and Nutrition Calculations

- Ingredients used for testing represent those that the majority of consumers use in their homes: large eggs, 2% milk, 80%-lean ground beef, canned ready-to-use chicken broth and vegetable oil spread containing not less than 65 percent fat.

- Fat-free, low-fat or low-sodium products were not used, unless otherwise indicated.

- Solid vegetable shortening (not butter, margarine, nonstick cooking sprays or vegetable oil spread as they can cause sticking problems) was used to grease pans, unless otherwise indicated.

Equipment Used in Recipe Testing

We use equipment for testing that the majority of consumers use in their homes. If a specific piece of equipment (such as a wire whisk) is necessary for recipe success, it is listed in the recipe.

- Cookware and bakeware without nonstick coatings were used, unless otherwise indicated.

- No dark-colored, black or insulated bakeware was used.

- When a pan is specified in a recipe, a metal pan was used; a baking dish or pie plate means ovenproof glass was used.

- An electric hand mixer was used for mixing only when mixer speeds are specified in the recipe directions. When a mixer speed is not given, a spoon or fork was used.

Cooking Terms Glossary

Beat: Mix ingredients vigorously with spoon, fork, wire whisk, hand beater or electric mixer until smooth and uniform.

Boil: Heat liquid until bubbles rise continuously and break on the surface and steam is given off. For rolling boil, the bubbles form rapidly.

Chop: Cut into coarse or fine irregular pieces with a knife, food chopper, blender or food processor.

Cube: Cut into squares ½ inch or larger.

Dice: Cut into squares smaller than ½ inch.

Grate: Cut into tiny particles using small rough holes of grater (citrus peel or chocolate).

Grease: Rub the inside surface of a pan with shortening, using pastry brush, piece of waxed paper or paper towel, to prevent food from sticking during baking (as for some casseroles).

Julienne: Cut into thin, matchlike strips, using knife or food processor (vegetables, fruits and meats).

Mix: Combine ingredients in any way that distributes them evenly.

Sauté: Cook foods in hot oil or margarine over medium-high heat with frequent tossing and turning motion.

Shred: Cut into long, thin pieces by rubbing food across the holes of a shredder, as for cheese, or by using a knife to slice very thinly, as for cabbage.

Simmer: Cook in liquid just below the boiling point on top of the stove; usually after reducing heat from a boil. Bubbles will rise slowly and break just below the surface.

Stir: Mix ingredients until uniform consistency. Stir once in a while for stirring occasionally, often for stirring frequently and continuously for stirring constantly.

Toss: Tumble ingredients (such as green salad) lightly with a lifting motion, usually to coat evenly or mix with another food.

metric conversion guide

VOLUME

U.S. UNITS	CANADIAN METRIC	AUSTRALIAN METRIC
¼ teaspoon	1 mL	1 ml
½ teaspoon	2 mL	2 ml
1 teaspoon	5 mL	5 ml
1 tablespoon	15 mL	20 ml
¼ cup	50 mL	60 ml
⅓ cup	75 mL	80 ml
½ cup	125 mL	125 ml
⅔ cup	150 mL	170 ml
¾ cup	175 mL	190 ml
1 cup	250 mL	250 ml
1 quart	1 liter	1 liter
1½ quarts	1.5 liters	1.5 liters
2 quarts	2 liters	2 liters
2½ quarts	2.5 liters	2.5 liters
3 quarts	3 liters	3 liters
4 quarts	4 liters	4 liters

WEIGHT

U.S. UNITS	CANADIAN METRIC	AUSTRALIAN METRIC
1 ounce	30 grams	30 grams
2 ounces	55 grams	60 grams
3 ounces	85 grams	90 grams
4 ounces (¼ pound)	115 grams	125 grams
8 ounces (½ pound)	225 grams	225 grams
16 ounces (1 pound)	455 grams	500 grams
1 pound	455 grams	½ kilogram

MEASUREMENTS

INCHES	CENTIMETERS
1	2.5
2	5.0
3	7.5
4	10.0
5	12.5
6	15.0
7	17.5
8	20.5
9	23.0
10	25.5
11	28.0
12	30.5
13	33.0

TEMPERATURES

FAHRENHEIT	CELSIUS
32°	0°
212°	100°
250°	120°
275°	140°
300°	150°
325°	160°
350°	180°
375°	190°
400°	200°
425°	220°
450°	230°
475°	240°
500°	260°

NOTE: The recipes in this cookbook have not been developed or tested using metric measures. When converting recipes to metric, some variations in quality may be noted.

index

Note: *Italicized* page references indicate photographs.